Some Emigrants to Virginia

SECOND EDITION, ENLARGED

MEMORANDA IN REGARD TO SEVERAL HUNDRED
EMIGRANTS TO VIRGINIA DURING THE
COLONIAL PERIOD WHOSE PARENT-
AGE IS SHOWN OR FORMER
RESIDENCE INDICATED
BY AUTHENTIC
RECORDS

COMPILED BY

W. G. STANARD

CLEARFIELD

Reprinted for
Clearfield Company, Inc. by
Genealogical Publishing Co., Inc.
Baltimore, Maryland
1992, 1993, 1994, 1995, 1998, 2003

Originally published: Richmond, Virginia, ca. 1911
Second Edition, Enlarged: Richmond, 1915
Reprinted: Southern Book Company
Baltimore, 1953
Reissued: Genealogical Publishing Co., Inc.
Baltimore, 1964, 1972, 1976, 1979, 1988
Library of Congress Catalogue Card Number 64-19875
International Standard Book Number 0-8063-0320-4
Made in the United States of America

PREFACE

The following list was begun during leisure hours with the expectation that it would be very much shorter than it is, and without any special idea of publication. After some progress had been made the compiler grew interested in ascertaining how many such instances could be discovered in readily accessible sources, and when it was completed it was thought that, though it consisted only of brief memoranda, it was probably worth preserving in print.

No attempt has before been made to collect the names of the various emigrants to Virginia in regard to whose parentage, family connections, or former homes something definite could be learned. In the list here presented there is no claim for exhaustiveness, nor is there any attempt to give many details as to ancestry, social position, or occupation. It is a list of names with brief notes concerning them, and with references to printed books or manuscripts, where proofs of the statements made are either given in full or epitomized. It is not intended as an enumeration of gentry, but includes all ranks from the laborer to the lord.

Though of use, no doubt, for genealogical investigations, the compilation was not made for that purpose; but to give examples of the great variety of people who composed the emigrants to the old colonies.

Some of the persons, whose names are given, died without issue, others returned to England, and of still others nothing is known but the name. Yet they all lived in Virginia, and with their different characters, habits, and antecedents helped to make the colony what it was and to mould the character of the Virginia people.

The principal sources used have been the *Virginia Magazine of History and Biography* (cited as V. M.), the *William and Mary Quarterly* (cited as W. M.), *Waters' Gleanings* (cited as

3

W. G), the *New England Historical and Genealogical Register*, various other well-known genealogical and biographical works, and a large collection of manuscript notes from Virginia county records in the possession of the compiler. In the *Virginia Magazine of History and Biography* Mr. Lothrop Withington's "Gleanings" have furnished numerous names.

In many instances, where there has been no opportunity for minute investigation, only one year of an emigrant's residence in Virginia has been noted. The name of the emigrant is first given, followed next by his dates, and immediately after this the place of his residence in Virginia, and finally the foreign reference. When details as to ancestry are given in the authorities referred to, as in the case of John West, Edward Digges, and many others, it has not been deemed necessary to add the social designation of gentleman, esquire, &c. This has been only done, as a rule, in cases where contemporary records affix such titles to the emigrant's name and the compiler knew nothing of his ancestry.

In conclusion, it should be said that no statements have been made for which it is believed there is not full proof in reliable records. All probabilities, however strong or reasonable, and all merely traditional accounts have been omitted. This is also the case in regard to some positive statements as to parentage or descent for which no authority has been given.

It will be observed that many prominent Virginia names are omitted from this list. The emigrant ancestors of the families of Alexander, Berkeley (Middlesex, &c.), Braxton, Brockenbrough, Brooke, Carter, Chew, Cocke (of Henrico, Surry, &c.), Dandridge, Eppes, Farrar, Jefferson, Grymes (Middlesex), Harrison (Surry, &c.), Harwood, Hooe, Kenner, Kennon, Lee, Madison, Marshall, Mason, Newton (Norfolk), Perrott, Pettus, Pope, Poythress, Rootes, Ruffin, Slaughter, Steptoe, Stith, Swann, Taliaferro, Venable, Walke, Whiting, Willoughby (Norfolk), and many other well-known names have not been traced positively to their former homes across the sea. It has been only recently that any work has been done towards this end in the English records, and it is hoped that many more details will yet be discovered.

Note to Second Edition

The first edition of this little book was exhausted early in 1915, and there has since been sufficient demand for it to justify the printing of another. Some necessary corrections and alterations have been made in the text of the first edition, and through information obtained since its publication the compiler has been able to add a number of emigrants to the list first given.

He wishes to express here his great obligation to two men who have died since the first publication of this pamphlet—Henry F. Waters and Lothrop Withington. The former, in ripe old age, peacefully in his home; the latter, in the prime of life, lost on the *Lusitania*.

Some Emigrants to Virginia

ABBES, EDWARD, surgeon (d. 1637), formerly of London.
V. M., XIV, 442. Mathews' Probate Acts.

ABRAHALL, ROBERT (in Virginia 1681, &c.), New Kent
county. In 1681, Richard Cawthorn and Ann his wife, adminis-
tratrix of her late husband, Thomas Abrahall, citizen and skinner, of London, gave a power of attorney to recover property
in the hands of Mr. Robert Abrahall, of New Kent county, Va.
A deed from the latter to Wm. Bassett bears on the seal the arms
of Abrahall of Herefordshire.
Middlesex Records.

ADAM, ROBERT (b. 1731), Alexandria; son of Rev. John
Adam, D. D., and Janet Campbell, his wife, of Kirkbride,
Scotland.
"The Lodge of Washington," p. 73.

ADAMS, EBENEZER (d. 1735), New Kent county; son of
Richard Adams, of Abridge, Essex, citizen and merchant tailor
of London.
W. M., V, 159-161.

ADAMS, THOMAS (in Virginia shortly before 1664), Isle of
Wight county; brother of William Adams, of Kenton, Devon.
W. M., VII, 225.

ALLAN, JOHN (d. 1750), Spotsylvania county, merchant,
formerly of Hamilton, Scotland, and son of James Allan, merchant, Baillie of Hamilton.
Spotsylvania Records, p. 186.

AMBLER, RICHARD (1690-1766), Yorktown and Jamestown;
son of John and Elizabeth (Burkadike) Ambler, of the city of
York.
Paxton's "Marshall Family," p. 42.

ANDREWS, HENRY, gentleman (d. 1705), formerly of London.
W. M., II, 165.

ANDREWS, JOHN (d. in or before 1609); son of John Andrews,
of Cambridge, merchant.
V. M., XI, 155.

ARCHER, MICHAEL, gentleman (1681-1726), James City
county; born near Rippon, in Yorkshire.
Va. Hist. Col., VI, 71.

ASCOUGH or AYSCOUGH, HENRY, gent. (b. about 1649, in
Virginia 1679-1698, &c.), Henrico county; brother of William
Ascough, of the city of York (alive 1716).
Henrico County Records.

ASHTON, PETER (d. 1671), Northumberland and Stafford
counties; brother of James Ashton, of Kirby-Underwood, and
of John Ashton, of Lowth (Louth), both in Lincolnshire.
V. M., II, 27.

ASHTON, JAMES (d. 1686), Stafford county, formerly of
Kirby-Underwood, Lincolnshire.
V. M., II, 27; X, 292.

ASHTON, JOHN (d. 1682), Stafford county, formerly of Lowth
(Louth), Lincolnshire.
V. M., X, 293.

ATKINS, JOHN (d. 1624), James City county; brother of Wil-
liam Atkins, who, in 1624, dwelt near the Bear, in Bassinghall,
London.
V. M., XI, 153.

ATKINS, JOHN (in Virginia 1636); grandson of John Atkins,
of Chard, Somerset, merchant.
V. M., XI, 150.

ATKINSON, ROGER (1725-1784), Blandford, Prince George
county; born at Whitehaven; son of Roger and Jane (Benson)
Atkinson.
V. M., XV, 345.

ATKINSON, WILLIAM, the younger, gent. (d. 1613), formerly of London; son of William Atkinson, of London, Esq.

V. M., XII, 397.

ATTERBURY, RICHARD (d. 1638), formerly of London, fishmonger.

V. M., XI, 153.

ATWOOD, JAMES (d. 1686), Middlesex county, formerly of Yorkshire.

Ch. Ch. Middlesex Parish Register.

BACON, MRS. ELIZABETH (in Virginia 1674, &c.), Henrico county; wife of Nathaniel Bacon, Jr., and daughter of Sir Edward Duke, of Benhill Lodge, near Saxmundham, Suffolk.

Campbell's "History of Virginia," 312; V. M., XV, 65, 69.

BACON, NATHANIEL, SR. (1620-1692), York county; son of Rev. James Bacon, Rector of Burgate, Suffolk, and grandson of Sir James Bacon, of Freston Hall, Suffolk.

V. M., II, 125, 129.

BACON, NATHANIEL, JR. (1647-1676), Henrico county; son of Thomas Bacon, of Freston Hall, near Saxmundham, Suffolk.

W. M., X, 267.

BAGGE, EDMUND (d. 1734), Essex county; son of Luke Bagge, of Start, county Waterford, Ireland.

V. M., XII, 290-300.

BAGGE, REV. JOHN (d. 1726), Essex county; brother of Leonard Bagge, of Kilbree, county Waterford, Ireland.

V. M., XII, 299-300.

BAGWELL, ROGER (d. 1679), Rappahannock county; brother of Andrew Bagwell, of Apson, county of Devon.

"Virginia County Records" (New York), p. 215.

BAKER, JOHN (in Virginia 1653), Lower Norfolk county; son and heir of John Baker, "of St. Martin's in the Fields in the county of Middlesex, near London" (dead in 1653). John Baker, Jr., refers to property in that parish and in "Benfield towards Windsor."

Lower Norfolk Records.

BAKER, MARTIN (in Virginia 1635, &c.), York county; formerly of Plymouth.

V. M., II, 240.

BANKS, THOMAS (1642-1697), Northumberland county; born at Woodstock, Wiltshire; son of Thomas Banks, gent., and Dorothy his wife.

W. M., XIII, 46.

BANKES, JAMES (in Virginia 1656, &c.), Lower Norfolk county; formerly of London, merchant.

Lower Norfolk Records.

BANTON, JOHN (in Virginia 1669, &c.), Isle of Wight county; formerly of Bristol, merchant.

Isle of Wight Records.

BARGRAVE, REV. THOMAS (d. 1621); son of Robert Bargrave, of Bridge, Kent.

Brown's "Genesis," II, 823.

BARNABE, JOHN (in Virginia 1631, &c.); brother of Richard Barnabe, merchant, of London.

V. M., XIII, 303-305.

BARNES, JACOB (in Virginia 1677, &c.); son of Edward Barnes and brother of Joshua Barnes, Greek Professor at Cambridge.

V. M., XVI, 203.

BASKERVILLE, JOHN (d. 1675), York county; son of John Baskerville, Esq., of Old Withington, Cheshire.

V. M., XV, 58-60.

BASSETT, WILLIAM (d. 1672), New Kent county; son of William Bassett, yeoman, of Newport, Isle of Wight. He had been an officer in the English garrison at Dunkirk (probably in Alsop's regiment) until it was evacuated in 1662.

Keith's "Ancestry of Benjamin Harrison," 27-29

BATH, JOHN (in Virginia 1623), "of London; a Leather-seller."

V. M., XIX, 133.

BATTE, HENRY (in Virginia 1660, &c.); son of Robert Batte, Vice-Master of University College, Oxford.

Rd. Standard, III, 40. Genealogist, October, 1898, 86-89.

BATTE, WILLIAM (in Virginia 1654, &c.); Charles City county; brother of Henry Batte, preceding.

Richmond Standard, III, 40.

BATTE, THOMAS (in Virginia 1666, &c.); son of John Batte (d. 1652), of Okewell, Yorkshire, and his wife, Martha, daughter of Thomas Mallory, Dean of Chester.

Rd. Standard, III, 40. Genealogist, October, 1898, 85-89.

BATTE, HENRY (in Virginia 1666, &c.), Charles City county; brother of Thomas Batte, preceding.

Rd. Standard, III, 40. Genealogist, October, 1898, 86-89.

BATHURST, LANCELOT (b. 1646), New Kent county; son of Sir Edward Bathurst, Bart., of Lechlade, Gloucestershire (who d. 1674).

Visitation of Gloucestershire (Exeter, 1884). W. M., II, 215. Burke's Extinct and Dormant Baronetage.

BAUGH, THOMAS, "absent in Virginia," 1634. (*Visitation of the County of Worcester*, 1683-84, ed. by W. C. Metcalfe), living at "West and Shirley Hundred," 1623, and at the "College Land" (Henrico), 1625. Son of John Baugh and grandson of Rowland Baugh, Esq., of Twining, in the county of Worcester.

Visitation of Worcestershire, 1683-84, edited by W. C. Metcalfe (Exeter, 1883). V. M., VII, 424.

BAUGH, WILLIAM (in Virginia 1639, &c.), late of London. (Probably William Baugh, who was born in 1610, and was J. P. for Henrico county, 1656, &c.)

V. M., XIX, 193.   11

BAYLY, ARTHUR (in Virginia 1642, &c.), Henrico county; of London, merchant.
Col. Va. Register. V. M.

BAYNES, THOMAS (d. 1709), Middlesex county; brother of William and Christopher Baynes, of Snape, Yorkshire.
Middlesex Records.

BAYTOP, THOMAS (d. 1690), Gloucester county; from Staplehurst, Kent.
V. M., XI, 69.

BEARD, WILLIAM (d. 1636), James City county; mentions in his will his sisters in Rye.
V. M., XI, 148.

BEAUCHAMP, JOHN (d. 1668), Henrico county; also of St. Giles Without Cripplegate, London, merchant; brother of Abel Beauchamp, gentleman, of Worcester.
V. M., XVI, 192. Henrico Records.

BECHINOE, EDWARD (in Virginia 1668, &c.), Isle of Wight county; brother of Conyers Bechinoe, of London, merchant.
W. M., VII, 226.

BECKINGHAM, ROBERT (d. 1675), Lancaster county; names in will his father, Mr. Robert Beckingham; sister Martha, wife of Mr. John Burroughs; brothers-in-law John Cume and Aubin Elves, and gives £8 sterling to the poor housekeepers in the parish of St. Edmund's, in Sarum. In 1669 was "of Portsmouth [Eng.], merchant."
Lancaster Records.

BECKWITH, SIR MARMADUKE, BART. (in Virginia 1709, &c., d. 1780), Richmond county; son of Sir Roger Beckwith, Bart., of Aldborough, Yorkshire (who d. 1700).
Burke's Extinct and Dormant Baronetage. Richmond County Records.

BEDFORD, JOHN (d. 1716), York county; of Stepney, Middlesex.
V. M., XI, 150.

BEHEATHLAND, JOHN (d. 1639); from St. Endillion, Cornwall; grandson of Mr. Richard Beheathland.
V. M., XI, 363. Matthews' Probate Acts.

BELCHES, HUGH (1737-1803), Sussex county; son of Thomas Belches, of Greenyard, Scotland, and his wife, Margaret Hepburn, of Boards.
Belches' Family Records.

BELCHES, JAMES, Surry county; brother of Hugh Belches, preceding.
Belches' Family Records.

BELCHES, PATRICK (1733-1766), Hanover county; brother of Hugh Belches, preceding.
Belches' Family Records.

BENNETT, RICHARD (d. 1675), Nansemond county; nephew of Edward Bennett, merchant, of London, who, in 1621, &c., was deputy governor of the merchant adventurers of England, resident at Delft, Holland.
Virginia Carolorum, 224, &c.

BENSKIN, HENRY (in Virginia 1691, &c.); son of Francis Benskin, Esq., of St. Martin's in the Fields, Middlesex.
Waters' Gleanings.

BERKELEY, JOHN (d. 1622), Henrico county; son of Sir John Berkeley, of Beverstone Castle, Gloucestershire.
W. M., VI, 135.

BERNARD, RICHARD (in Virginia 1655, &c.), Gloucester county; in 1634 was of Petsoe, Bucks, gent.
W. M., III, 41.

BERNARD, WILLIAM (d. 1665), Nansemond county; son of Francis Bernard, of Kingsthorpe, Northants (d. 1630), and brother of Sir Robert Bernard, Bart., of Brampton Hall, Huntingdonshire.
V. M., IV, 207.

BEVERLEY, ROBERT (d. 1687), Middlesex county; a native of Yorkshire.

Ch. Ch. Parish, Middlesex, Register. V. M., II, 405-413.

BICKLEY, FRANCIS (in Virginia 1657, &c.); son of John Bickley, of London, draper.

V. M., XI, 151, 152.

BICKLEY, JOSEPH (d. before 1751), King William county; son of Sir Francis Bickley, Bart., of Attleborough Hall, Norfolk. (Joseph Bickley's son William, of Louisa county, succeeded to the baronetcy in 1752.)

W. M., V, 29-30, 124-125.

BIGGE, HENRY (in Virginia 1635, &c.); brother of John Bigge, of St. Mary's, White Chapel, London, citizen and tallow-chandler.

Waters' Gleanings.

BILLINGSLEY, GEORGE (d. 1681), Upper Norfolk county; refers in will to property left him by his grandmother, Agatha Billingsley, of Rotterdam.

Maryland Calendar of Wills, I, 149.

BISHOP, HENRY (in Virginia 1646, &c.), Surry county; of Henfield, Sussex; was Postmaster General of England 1660-63.

V. M., VIII, 330. Virginia Carolorum.

BLACKBURN, RICHARD (1705-1757), Prince William county; born at Rippon, Yorkshire.

W. M., IV, 267.

BLACKEY, THOMAS (in Virginia 1686, &c.), Middlesex county; of Cumberland.

Ch. Ch. Parish, Middlesex, Register.

BLANCHEFLOWER, BENJAMIN (d. 1684-85 in Virginia), "of Fitzhead, county of Somerset, Gent."

V. M., XIX, 186.

14

BLAND, GILES (1647-1676), Charles City county; son of John Bland, of London, and his wife Sarah, daughter of Giles Green, Esq., of Uffington, in the Isle of Purbeck.

Familiæ Minorum Gentium.

BLAND, EDWARD (d. 1664), Charles City county; son of John Bland, of London, merchant.

W. M., XV, 47. Familiæ Minorum Gentium.

BLAND, THEODERICK (1629-1671), Charles City county; son of John Bland, of London, merchant.

V. M., X, 372, 373. Familiæ Minorum Gentium.

BLOSS, JOHN (in Virginia 1687, &c.), Middlesex county; of Colchester, Essex.

Ch. Ch., Middlesex, Parish Register.

BOLITHOE, JOHN (in Virginia 1725, &c.), Princess Anne county; from Cornwall.

Lower Norfolk County (Va.) Antiquary, I, 64.

BOLLING, ROBERT (1646-1709), Charles City and Prince George counties; son of John and Mary Bolling of All Hallows, Barking Parish, Tower street, London.

V. M., VII, 352, 353.

BOLTON, HENRY (in Virginia 1691, &c.); son of William Bolton, clerk of Harrow on the Hill, Middlesex.

W. G., 662.

BOOTH, HUMPHREY (in Virginia 1654, &c.), Rappahannock county, of London, merchant, in 1653.

V. M., III, 66.

BOOTH, THOMAS (1662-1736), Gloucester county; "born in Lancashire" (epitaph). A chart pedigree of the family, prepared many years ago, states that he was son of St. John Booth, son of John Booth, son of Sir George Booth, whose son William was the father of the first Lord Delamere.

W. M., II, 223, 273, 274.

BOUCHER, REV. JONATHAN (b. 1738), Caroline county; a native of Cumberland.

Meade, I, 411.

BOWKER, REV. JAMES (d. 1704), New Kent county; brother of Edward Bowker, of London.

V. M., XI, 313.

BOWKER, REV. RALPH (in Virginia 1704, &c.), King and Queen county; brother of Rev. James Bowker, preceding.

V. M., XI, 313.

BOYD, DAVID (d. 1781), Northumberland county; his father and mother were buried in the churchyard at Wigton, Scotland.

W. M., VII, 126.

BRADFORD, THOMAS (d. 1671); formerly of Batcombe, Somerset.

P. C. C. Act Book.

BRADLEY, THOMAS (b. 1633), a merchant in Virginia 1665, eldest son of Thomas Bradley, D. D., chaplain to Charles I, Prebend of York and Rector of Ackworth, Yorkshire; a great Royalist, and his wife Frances, daughter of John, Lord Saville, of Pontefract.

Genealogist (new series), XVI, 117.

BRANCH, CHRISTOPHER (d. 1681), Henrico county; son of Lionel Branch (b. 1566, d. about 1605), and grandson of William Branch, gent. (d. 1602), of Abingdon, Berkshire.

MS. pedigree prepared by Mr. J. H. Lea.

BRAY, ROBERT (d. 1681), Lower Norfolk county; son of Edward Bray, of Biggleswade, Bedfordshire (who was dead in 1681).

Lower Norfolk Records.

BRAY, PLOMER (in Virginia 1681, &c.), Lower Norfolk county; brother of Robert Bray, preceding.

Lower Norfolk Records.

BRENT, GEORGE (d. 1700), Stafford county; son of George Brent, of Defford, Worcestershire, and his wife Marianna, daughter of Sir John Peyton, of Doddington.

V. M., II, 35, 36; XII, 441; XIV, 100, 101; XV, 93, 94.

BRENT, GILES (d. 1671), Stafford county; son of Richard Brent, of Lark Stoke and Admington, Gloucestershire.

V. M., XII, 439-440; XIV, 100; XV, 324, &c.; XVI, 97, 98.

BRENT, ROBERT (in Virginia 1693, &c.); son of George Brent, of Defford.

V. M., XIV, 101.

BREWER, JOHN (d. 1636), Warwick county; son of Thomas Brewer, of London.

W. G., 715; V. M., III, 183, 184.

BREWSTER, SACKFORD (in Virginia 1655, &c.), Surry county. In his marriage license, issued in Virginia, April 22, 1655, he is styled "Thomas alias Sackford Brewster, of Sackford Hall, in the county of Suffolk, gent."

Surry Records.

BREWTON, JOHN (d. 1707), Stafford county; legacy in his will to John, son of Thomas Brewton, of Gloucester, in England.

Stafford Records.

BRIGG, HENRY (in Virginia 1622, &c.); brother to "Thomas Brigg, merchant at ye Custome House Key," London.

Brown's "First Republic," p. 514.

BRISTOW, ROBERT (in Virginia 1660-80, b. 1643), Stafford county; second son of Robert Bristow, Esq., of Ayot St. Lawrence, Hertfordshire.

V. M., XIII, 59-62.

BRITAIN, RICHARD (in Virginia 1659, &c.), Northampton county; son of Stephen Britain, of East Greenwich, in the county of Kent, cordwainer.

Northampton Records.

17

BROADHURST, JOHN, "the younger, of London, factor" (d. 1701), Princess Anne county; in will, date September 13, 1699, bequeaths real estate "at Hoesfield near Macksfield in the county of Chester." Probate Act P. C. C. "John Broadhurst of St. Albans, Wood street, London, but in Virginia deceased."
Princess Anne County Records.

BRODHURST, HUGH (d. 1659); son of William Brodhurst, gent., of Lilleshall, Shropshire.
W. M., IV, 88.

BRODHURST, WALTER (1619-1661), Westmoreland county; brother of Hugh Brodhurst, preceding.
W. M., IV, 31, 74, 88; I, 188.

BRODNAX, JOHN (d. 1657), York county; son of Thomas Brodnax, of Godmersham, Kent.
W. M., XIV, 52-53.

BRODNAX, JOHN (1668-1719), Williamsburg; son of Robert Brodnax, goldsmith, of Holborn, London.
W. M., XIV, 138.

BRODNAX, WILLIAM (1675-1726), Jamestown; born at Godmersham, Kent; son of "Robert Brodnax, a goldsmith in Holborn, London."
W. M., XIV, 53-56.

BROUGHTON, FRANCIS, "now in Virginia"; pedigree of Broughton, Visitation of Staffordshire, 1663-4.
W. M., XV, 70.

BROWN, DR. JOHN (d. 1726), Williamsburg; "late of Cold Stream, North Britain."
Va. Hist. Col., VI, 76; W. M., VI, 253.

BUCKRIDGE, RALPH (in Virginia 1623); "of Sutten, in Barkshire, gent."
V. M., XIX, 132.

BURWELL, MRS. ABIGAIL (in Virginia 1671, &c.), Gloucester county; wife of Lewis Burwell, and daughter of Anthony Smith, of Colchester, tanner, and his wife Martha, daughter of Rev. James Bacon, Rector of Burgate, Suffolk.

Keith's Ancestry of Benjamin Harrison, 23-26.

BURWELL, LEWIS (d. 1653), Gloucester county; son of Edward Burwell, of Harlington, Bedfordshire, and his wife Dorothy, daughter of William Bedell, of Catworth, Huntingdonshire.

Keith's Ancestry of Benjamin Harrison, 34, 35.

BUTLER, WILLIAM (in Virginia 1641, &c.), fishmonger, of London.

N. E. H. & G. Reg., Vol. 61, p. 92.

BUTTS, PETER (in Virginia 1672, &c.),York county; "late of London, merchant."

York County Records.

BYRD, WILLIAM (1652-1704), Henrico and Charles City counties; son of John Byrd, goldsmith, of London. Pedigrees prepared in London in 1702 and 1763 trace John Byrd's ancestry to the Byrds of Brexton, Cheshire.

Pedigree in "Writings of Col. Wm. Byrd" (Bassett ed.), and in "Beau Monde" (Richmond, April 7, 1894).

CABELL, DR. WILLIAM (1700-1774), Goochland and Amherst counties; son of Nicholas Cabell, of Frome, Somerset.

Cabells and Their Kin, 19-21, 63, &c.

CADE, HENRY (in Virginia 1662, &c.); son of Walter Cade, who was nephew of Andrew Cade, Esq., of East Betchworth, Surrey (who died in 1662).

V. M., XII, 71.

CAIRON, REV. JEAN (d. 1716), Henrico county; formerly minister of Cajarc, France.

Huguenot Emigration, 74.

CALTHORPE, CHRISTOPHER (d. 1662), York county; son of Christopher Calthorpe, Esq., of Blakeney, and brother of James Calthorpe, Esq., of East Barsham, Suffolk.

W. M., II, 106-112, 166-164.

CALVERT, WILLIAM (d. 1666), York county; had a brother, George Calvert, living near Newark, Nottinghamshire, and another brother, Fulke.
York County Records.

CAMM, REV. JOHN (1718-1779), York county; son of Thomas Camm, of Hornsea, Yorkshire.
W. M., IV, 61.

CAMPBELL, REV. ARCHIBALD (in Virginia 1754, &c.), Westmoreland county; son of Archibald Campbell, of Kirnan, Argyleshire, Scotland, and his wife Anna Stewart, of Ascog.
Rd. Standard, April 12 and May 3, 1879.

CAMPBELL, ALEXANDER (1710-1801), Falmouth; brother of Rev. Archibald Campbell, preceding. He returned to Scotland, and was father of Thomas Campbell, the poet.
Rd. Standard, April 12 and May 3, 1879.

CAMPFIELD, FRANCIS (in Virginia 1662, &c.), Gloucester county; citizen and grocer, of London.
V. M., XI, 307.

CARPENTER, NATHANIEL, King and Queen county, 1766, &c.; "A Devonshire gentleman," brother of Coryndon Carpenter, Esq., of Launceston, Cornwall.
Wallace's Virginia Historical Magazine—note to "Fauntleroy Family."

CARTER, EDWARD (d. 1682), of Nansemond county, Va.; returned to England, and at time of death was "of Edmonton county, Middlesex, Esq."; bequeathed lands in Edmonton and in Chalfont St. Peter's, county Bucks; to be buried in St. Dunston's in the East, London, near his former wife, Amie Carter.
Waters' Gleanings.

CARY, JOHN (b. 1644, living in Surry county, Va., 1669, &c., but of London in 1700); son of Thomas Cary, of Bristol.
N. E. H. & G. Reg.

CARY, MILES (1620-1667), Warwick county; son of John and Alice (Hobson) Cary, of Bristol.
Goode's "Virginia Cousins," 281-282.

CARY, OSWALD (in Virginia 1690, &c.), Middlesex county; son of James Cary, merchant, of London.
W. M., IX, 45.

CARY, WARREN (in Virginia 1711, &c.), Richmond county; brother of Richard Cary, of Bristol.
Richmond County Records.

CATLETT, JOHN (d. 1670), Sittingbourne Parish, Rappahannock county. His son, John Catlett, gave power of attorney to sell lands at Sittingbourne and Radwlesham(?), Kent, which had been left him by his father.
V. M., III, 62, 63.

CAWSON, JONAS (in Norfolk county, Va., about 1702, &c.); went to school in the town of Lancaster in 1692. His father lived a short distance from that town.
Norfolk County Records.

CAWTHORNE, RICHARD (in Virginia 1681, &c.), Rappahannock county; son of Richard Cawthorne, citizen and merchant-tailor, of London, whose wife, in 1681, was Anne, formerly widow of Thomas Abrahall, citizen and skinner, of London.
Middlesex Records.

CHAMBERLAYNE, THOMAS (in Virginia 1675, &c.), Henrico and Charles City counties; son of Col. Edmund Chamberlayne, of Maugersbury, Gloucestershire.
Visitation of Gloucestershire, 1682-3.

CHAMBERLAYNE, WILLIAM (1699 or 1700-1736), New Kent county; "Descended of an Ancient and Worthy Family in the County of Hereford" (epitaph).
Beau Monde, March 31, 1894.

CHANDLER, DANIEL (in Virginia 1650, &c.); son of Edward Chandler, of Ware, Hertfordshire, draper.
V. M., XIII, 309.

CHAPMAN, RICHARD (in Virginia 1740, &c.), King William county; from Lincolnshire.
W. M., VI, 60.

CHEESMAN, JOHN (d. 1665), Elizabeth City and York counties; at the time of his death "of St. Mary Magdalen, Bermondsey, Surrey, gent."; left property at Braban (Brabourne?), Kent, and at Southall, Eling, Old Bradford and New Bradford.
V. M., XIV, 86.

CHESLEY, PHILIP (d. 1674), York county; a native of Welford, Gloucestershire.
W. M., I, 86. V. M., XIII, 63.

CHEYNEY, HENRY (in Virginia 1623), "of York, merchant."
V. M., XIX, 133.

CHICHESTER, RICHARD (1657-1734), Lancaster county; born at Silverton, Devon, March 5, 1657; came to Virginia 1702; son of John Chichester of Widworthy (will 1661), whose great-great-grandfather, John Chichester of Widworthy, was a son of John Chichester of Raleigh.
Copies of wills, parish registers, &c., in possession of Mr. A. M. Chichester. Hayden's Virginia Genealogies, 93, &c.

CHICHLEY, SIR HENRY (1615-1683), Middlesex county; son of Sir Thomas Chichley, of Wimpole, Cambridgeshire.
V. M., April, 1909.

CHURCHILL, WILLIAM (1650-1711), Middlesex county; born at North Aston, Oxfordshire.
Keith's Ancestry of Benj. Harrison. W. M., VII, 186.

CLAIBORNE, WILLIAM (1587-1677), New Kent county, &c.; son of Edmund and Grace (Bellingham) Claiborne, of Kellerby, Yorkshire, and Cleborne Hall, Westmoreland.
V. M., I, 313.

CLACK, REV. JAMES (d. 1723), Gloucester county; born in the parish of Marden, Wiltshire; son of William and Mary Clack.
W. M., III, 32.

CLARKE, CHARLES (d. 1785), Cumberland and Powhatan counties; in Virginia 1745. Stated to have been a native of Surrey. In his will, dated 1763, he makes provision in case "the estate in England in the hands of my mother's sister, Mrs. Charity Kent, widow of Daniel Kent, merchant, formerly of Bell Court, Common Street, London," should be recovered.

Powhatan Records.

CLARKE, JOHN (d. shortly before 1644), York county; son of Sir John Clarke, of Wrotham, Kent.

W. M., I, 84, 85; XII, 36-37.

CLARKE, THOMAS (d. 1670), York county; son of Edward Clarke, of Thriploe, near Foulsmere, Cambridgeshire.

V. M., XII, 178.

CLAY, FRANCIS. In the "Prerogative Court of Mansfield" (a probate court now extinct, with the records at Nottingham), is the bond, dated March 3, 1691, of Daniel Clay, of Mansfield, joyner, as administrator of the goods of Francis Clay, "late of Chickahomene in Virginia." The inventory is filed with the bond and states that Francis Clay was the son of Richard Clay, deceased. The bond was given before William Clay, steward of the manor of Mansfield, who seals with his arms. A Francis Clay, gentleman, lived in Northumberland county, Va.; was a J. P. for that county 1659, &c., and in a deposition made in 1661, when he was aged thirty-four, says he came to Virginia in 1649.

N. E. H. & G. Reg., Vol. 37, p. 202. Northumberland County Records.

CLAYTON, JOHN (1665-1737), Gloucester county; son of Sir John Clayton, of London, and of Parsons Green, Fulham.

Wallace's Virginia Historical Magazine.

CLIFT, WOMBWELL (d. 1737), Hanover county; "of a good family in Yorkshire."

Virginia Gazette, January 10, 1737.

CLIFTON, JAMES (in Virginia 1669, &c.), Stafford county; son of Thomas Clifton, Esq., of Westby and Clifton, Lancashire.

Burke's Commoners (1835), II, 57, Md. Archives. Stafford County Records. V. M., XXII, 424, &c.; XXIII, 316, &c.

COCKE, MRS. ELIZABETH (in Virginia 1713, &c.), Williamsburg; wife of Dr. William Cocke, and sister of Mark Catesby, the English naturalist.

V. M., V, 189, 190; IX, 128.

COCKE, DR. WILLIAM (1672-1720), Williamsburg; "born of respectable parents at Sudbury in Suffolk." (Epitaph.)

Va. Hist. Col., VI, 84, 85.

CODD, ST. LEGER (d. 1708), Northumberland county; bequeathed lands at Wateringbury, Lenham, and Wetchlin (?), Kent. He was son of William Codd, Esq., of Pelicans, Kent, who married, in 1632, Mary, daughter of Sir Warham St. Leger, of Ulcombe, Kent.

V. M., X, 374; XXIII, 382.

COGGAN, MRS. FRANCES (d. 1677), Charles City county; wife of John Coggan, and daughter of Gregory Bland (b. 1587), of St. Gregories, London.

Familiæ Minorum Gentium. N. E. H. & G. Reg., Vol. 47, p. 354.

COKE, JOHN (1704-1767), Williamsburg; son of Richard Coke (d. 1730), and grandson of Richard Coke, of Trusley, Derbyshire.

Coke's "Coke of Trusley." W. M., VII, 127, 128.

COLCLOUGH, GEORGE (in Virginia 1658, &c.), Northumberland county; brother of Thomas Colclough, merchant, of London.

W. M., XVII, 60.

COLLIER, WILLIAM (in Virginia 1670, &c.), York and New Kent counties; formerly "citizen and weaver, of London."

W. M., VIII, 256.

COLE, WILLIAM (b. 1597, in Virginia 1618-29, &c.), Nutmeg Quarter; son of Humfrie Cole, of Tillingham, Essex, clerk.
V. M., XIX, 189, 190.

COLTMAN, HENRY (in Virginia 1622, &c.); son of Ann Coltman, of London, widow.
W. G., 141.

COLVILLE, JOHN (d. 1756), Fairfax county; late of Newcastle on Tyne; made bequests to his brother Thomas Colville, with reversion to the Earl of Tankerville, and states that the Earl was the son of his (J. C.'s) father's brother's daughter.
Fairfax County Records.

COLLINS, ROBERT (in Virginia 1623); "of London, haberdasher."
V. M., XIX, 133.

COMRIE, MRS. MARGARET (d. January 9, 1739); wife of Dr. William Comrie, of Hanover county; niece of Mr. Thomas Parratt, one of the Masters in Chancery (in England), and sister to Mr. Josias Baintone, one of the Six Clerks of that office.
Virginia Gazette, January 15, 1739.

CONWAY, EDWIN (d. 1675), Northampton and Lancaster counties; "of Worcestershire."
Hayden's Virginia Genealogies, 225-229.

CONSTABLE, ROBERT (in Virginia 1623), James City; "of North Allerton in Yorkshire, gent."
V. M., XIX, 133.

COOKE, TRAVERS (d. 1759), Stafford county; states in his will that there is a large balance due him from his uncle, Thomas Cooke, of Youghall, of the Kingdom of Ireland, on account of the rents and profits of his estate there.
Stafford Records.
(The will of Thomas Cooke, of Youghall, County Cork, gent., was proved in Dublin in 1750; that of John Cooke, of Youghal, Esq., proved in Dublin in 1713, and also a copy of the will of

John Cooke, of Overwharton parish, Stafford county, Va., the father of Travers Cooke, was proved in December, 1735.)

COOPER, SAMPSON (d. 1659), Northumberland county; Alderman of Rippon, Yorkshire.
W. M., XIII, 28.

CORBIN, HENRY (1629-1675), Middlesex county; third son of Thomas Corbin, Esq., of Hall End, Warwickshire.
"Lee of Virginia," 83. Corbin Pedigree. V. M., XVII, 401.

COSENS, JOHN (d. 1674), Northumberland county; came to Virginia from Cudredge (Goodrich ?) in the parish of Bishops Walton, Southampton, where he owned land.
Lancaster Records.

COTTON, WILLIAM, mariner, (in Virginia 1659, &c.); son of William Cotton, who owned a house at Bedminster near Bristol.
W. M., V, 124.

COTTON, REV. WILLIAM (d. 1646), Northampton county. His mother Joane lived at Bunbury, Cheshire.
V. M., IV, 406. W. M., V., 124.

CRABBE, JOHN (in Virginia 1675, &c.), Westmoreland county; brother of Osmond Crabbe, gent., of Brislington als Busselton, Somerset, who died 1695, and left to John Crabbe houses in Bristol, in the parish of Bedminster, Somerset, and at Brislington.
V. M., IX, 293, 294.

CRAMPTON, JOHN (in Virginia 1623), "of Bolton in the Moore, Lancashire."
V. M., XIX, 132.

CRAWLEY, THOMAS (in Virginia 1659, &c.), old Rappahannock county; son of Robert and Margaret Crawley, and baptized in the parish of St. Margaret's, Bristol, August 27, 1637.
Rappahannock Records.

CRISPE, THOMAS (in Virginia 1621-25), Elizabeth City; "of the Countie of Kent in England, gent."
V. M, XXIII, 1.

CROMPTON, THOMAS (in Virginia 1623), "of Bolton in the Moore, Lankashire."
V. M., XIX, 132.

CRAIK, DR. JAMES (1730-1784), Alexandria; son of William Craik, of Arbigland, near Dumfries, Scotland. (The father of John Paul Jones was a gardener at Arbigland.)
Hayden, 341.

CREFFIELD, EDWARD, JR. (d. 1694). Gloucester county; son of Edward Creffield, of Chapel, Essex.
V. M., XIX, 289.

CREYK, HENRY (1637-1684), Middlesex county; son of Gregory Creyk, of Marton, Yorkshire, and his wife Ursula, daughter of Sir John Legard.
Familiæ Minorum Gentium, III, 950-952. Genealogist (N. S., XXIII, 42). Middlesex Records.

CROUCH, RICHARD (b. about 1586, in Virginia 1623), James City county, "of Howton (Houghton) Bedfordshire, carpenter."
V. M., XIX, 133, 134.

CULPEPER, ALEXANDER (in Virginia 1672, &c.) In 1672 Governor Berkeley applied to the English Government for the appointment of his wife's brother, Alexander Culpeper, to the office of surveyor general of Virginia. He stated that Captain Culpeper was a person who had lived a number of years in Virginia, and whose father had lost his estate, liberty, and life in the King's service.
V. M., I, 83.

CURLE, THOMAS (1640-1700), Elizabeth City county; born in the parish of St. Michael, Lewis, Sussex.
W. M., IX, 125.

CUSTIS, EDMOND (in Virginia 1690, &c.), Northampton county; son of Francis Custis, of Baltimore, Ireland.
Northampton Records.

CUSTIS, JOHN (in Virginia 1650, &c.), Northampton county; son of John Custis, of Rotterdam, Holland, formerly of Gloucestershire, England.
V. M., VIII, 394.   27

CUSTIS, WILLIAM (in Virginia 1650, &c.), Northampton; brother of John Custis, preceding.

V. M., VIII, 394.

DADE, FRANCIS (d. 1663), Stafford county, 1654, &c.; sixth son of William Dade, Esq., of Tannington, Suffolk, and his wife Mary, daughter of Henry Wingfield, Esq., of Crofield, Suffolk. When Francis Dade came to Virginia he called himself for several years Major John Smith. The reason is unknown; but it was evidently nothing which prevented him from visiting England later, as he was returning from a visit to England when he died at sea in 1663.

Genealogical Memoranda Relating to the Family of Dade of Suffolk. Pedigrees from the Visitation of Kent, 1663-68, pp. 97, 98. Hayden's Virginia Genealogies, 731, &c. W. M., VIII, 205; V. M., XX, 210, &c., 323, &c.

DANIEL, THOMAS (in Virginia 1676, &c.); son of Ann Jones, widow, of St. Clements Danes, Middlesex.

W. G., 27.

DAVISON, CHRISTOPHER (d. before 1624), James City county; son of William Davison, of Middlesex, Secretary of State to Queen Elizabeth.

W. M., X, 169.

DAWSON, OWEN (in Virginia 1623), "of St. Martins in the Fields, joiner."

V. M., XIX, 132

DAWSON, MRS. ANNE (in Virginia 1744, &c.); wife of Benjamin Dawson, of Virginia, and sister of Francis Brooks, of Plaistow, Essex, gent.

V. M., XVI, 65.

DAWSON, REV. THOMAS (d. 1761), Williamsburg; son of William Dawson, "pleb." of Aspatria, Cumberland.

W. M., II, 209. Foster's Oxford Matriculations.

DAWSON, REV. MUSGRAVE (1723-   ), Caroline county; brother of Thomas Dawson, preceding.

W. M., II, 52.

DAWSON, REV. WILLIAM (d. 1752), Williamsburg; brother of Thomas Dawson, preceding.
W. M., II, 51.

DAVIS, JOHN (d. 1686), Middlesex county; of Bristol.
Ch. Ch., Middlesex, Parish Register.

DAVY, JOHN (in Virginia 1648, &c.); son of Simon Davy, and nephew of John Davy, gent., of Maidstone, Kent.
W. G., 1299.

DAY, JAMES (d. 1700), Isle of Wight county; owned two freehold tenements in Broadstreet in or near Augustine Fryers in the parish of St. Peter the Poor, London.
W. M., VII, 251.

DAYNES, WILLIAM (1617-   ), in Virginia (Lower Norfolk county) 1655; in 1679-80, of Bristol, merchant. In 1709 Sir William Daynes, of Bristol, made deeds in Norfolk county— though later than this a William Daynes, who died in Norfolk county.
Lower Norfolk and Norfolk Records.

DEANS, JAMES (d. 1762), Chesterfield county; left £200 to the Infirmary of Aberdeen.
Chesterfield Records.

DE GRAFFENREIDT, CHRISTOPHER, JR. (in Virginia 1722, &c.), Williamsburg and Prince George county; son of Baron Christopher De Graffenreidt, and Regina (Tscharner) his wife, of Berne, Switzerland.
W. M., XV, 61.

DELALUA, SOLOMON (d. 1703), Henrico county; late of Rochelle, France.

DENNET, WILLIAM (in Virginia 1641, &c.); fishmonger, of London.
N. E. H. & G. Reg., Vol. 61, p. 199.

DERICK, HENRY (d. 1677), late of the parish of St. Stephen's, Bristol.
V. M., XVI, 197, 198.

DEWALL, EDWARD (d. 1640), Warwicksqueake county; son of George Dewall, gent., of Reading, Berkshire. E. D., in his will, styles himself servant of Symon Cornocke, of Warwicksqueake, Va., and leaves his master an inn, called the Rose, in Reading, which had been left him by his father.
V. M., XIII, 204.

DEWS, RICHARD (d. 1686), Middlesex county; of Yorkshire. Ch. Ch., Middlesex, Parish Register.

DIGGES, EDWARD (1621-1676), York county; son of Sir Dudley Digges, of Chilham Castle, Kent; M. P. and Master of the Rolls, and his wife Mary, daughter and co-heiress of Sir Thomas Kempe, of Olantigh, Kent.
W. M., I, 87, 140, 141. Meade, I, 244. V. M., X, 378; XIV, 305.

DINWIDDIE, JOHN (d. 1726), King George county; son of Robert Dinwiddie, merchant of Glasgow, and brother of Robert Dinwiddie, Governor of Virginia.
Dinwiddie Papers, I, XXI-XXIII. King George Records.

DIXON, JOHN (in Virginia 1729-51, d. 1758), King and Queen county; at time of death was "of Bristol, Esquire," owned houses and land at Lateridge in the parish of Iron Acton, Gloucestershire.
V. M., July, 1911.

DOGGETT, REV. BENJAMIN (d. 1682), Lancaster county; had a brother Richard Doggett, of Ipswich, merchant.
Lancaster Records.

DONNALLY, JAMES (came to Virginia 1761, alive 1768), Greenbrier county; refers in a deposition to persons he had known at Belligay, Donegal, Ireland.
Abstracts of Records of Augusta County, II, 12, 13.

DONNE, GEORGE (in Virginia 1637, &c.); baptized May 9, 1605, at Camberwell, Surrey; son of Dr. John Donne.
Neill's Virginia Carolorum.

DORMER, SIR FLEETWOOD (in Virginia 1649, &c.); formerly of Arle Court, Gloucestershire; son of Sir Fleetwood Dormer, of Lee Grange and Purton, Bucks (who d. 1639).

Burke's Extinct and Dormant Baronetage. V. M., XIII, 406.

DOUGLAS, JAMES (1724-), Prince William county; son of James Campbell Douglas, of Mains, Scotland, and brother of Margaret (d. 1774), who married Archibald, Duke of Douglas.

Hayden, 691. V. M., XXII, 273, &c., 418.

DOUGLASS, WILLIAM (d. 1783), Loudoun county; son of Hugh Douglass, of Garalland or Garallan, parish of Old Cumnock, Scotland.

V. M., 336.

DOWNE, JANE (in Virginia 1653, &c.); niece of Nicholas Downe, of London, Esq. (She was probably a daughter of George Downe, or Downes, of Elizabeth City county, 1632, &c.)

V. M., XXII, 26.

DOWNES, JOHN (in Virginia 1623), "of London, grocer."

V. M., XIX, 133.

DOWTHWAITE, WILLIAM (d. 1659), York county; brother of Nicholas Dowthwaite, of Cliffords Inn, gent.

York County Records.

DOYLEY, REV. COPE (d. 1713), Williamsburg; son of Charles Doyley, gent., of Southrop, Gloucestershire.

V. M., XII, 300, 301.

DUNCANSON, ROBERT (d.), Fredericksburg; brother of Thos. Duncanson, surgeon, of Forres, county of Murray, North Britain (alive 1764).

"Spotsylvania Records," p. 266.

DUNLOP, WILLIAM (1707-1739), Prince William county; son of Alexander Dunlop, Greek Professor in the University of Glasgow.

W. M., XV, 279.

DYER, JOHN (in Virginia 1623), "of London, carpenter."

V. M., XIX, 134.

EARLE, GEORGE (in Virginia 1637, &c.), Lower Norfolk county; son of George Earle, of Eastratford, Nottinghamshire, draper.
N. E. H. & G. Reg., Vol. 55, pp. 339, 340.

EELES, NATHANIEL (in Virginia 1618, &c.); son of Nathaniel Eeles, of Harpendon, Hertfordshire.

ELLIOTT, THOMAS (d. 1686), Middlesex county; of Chipping Ongar, Essex.
Ch. Ch., Middlesex, Parish Register.

EMAN, JOHN (in Virginia 1623), "of London, goldsmith."
V. M., XIX, 133.

EVELYN, GEORGE (1593-   ), in Virginia 1649, &c., James City county; son of Robert Evelyn, and grandson of George Evelyn, of Long Ditton, Surrey.
Scull's "Evelyns in America," 1-45. V. M., IX, 172.

EVELYN, MOUNTJOY (in Virginia about 1650, &c.), Northampton county; son of George Evelyn (preceding), and grandson of Robert Evelyn, of Long Ditton and Godstone, Surrey.
Scull's "Evelyns in America," 66. V. M., IX, 172, 173.

EVELYN, ROBERT (b. 1593, d. 1649), born in London, in Virginia 1637, &c.; youngest son of Robert Evelyn, of Long Ditton, Surrey.
Scull's "Evelyns in America," 47-59, 66.

FABIAN, SYMON (in Virginia 1668, &c.), lived on York River; son of Edmond Fabian, of St. Andrew's, Holborn, Middlesex, citizen and merchant tailor.
V. M., XV, 300.

FAIRFAX, FERDINANDO (1636-1664), in Virginia 1659, &c.; a Virginia merchant of London; son of Col. Charles Fairfax, of Menston, Yorkshire, and grandson of Thomas, first Baron Fairfax of Cameron.
Herald and Genealogist, VI, 401. V. M., VII, 73.

FAIRFAX, THOMAS, 6TH LORD (1690-1781), Frederick county.
Burke's Peerage.

FAIRFAX, WILLIAM (1691-1757), Fairfax county; son of Henry Fairfax, of Towlston, Yorkshire, and grandson of Henry, 4th Lord Fairfax. (W. F.'s son Bryan succeeded to the title.)
V. M., IV, 102, &c. "The Thomas Book," 308, 309.

FARLEY, THOMAS (in Virginia 1623, &c.), James City county; "of Worcester in Worcestershire, gent."
V. M., XIX, 131, 132.

FARNEFOLD, REV. JOHN (in Virginia 1672-1702), Northumberland county; son of Sir Thomas Farnefold, of Gatwickes in Stayning, Sussex.
W. M., XVII, 245.

FARNEFOLD, MRS. MARY, Northumberland county; wife of Rev. John Farnefold, and daughter of George Brookes, of London, merchant.
W. M., XVII, 245.

FARRINGTON, RICHARD (in Virginia 1677, &c.), Lancaster county; brother of John Farrington, of London, merchant.
Lancaster Records.

FAUNTLEROY, MOORE (-1663), Rappahannock county; son of John Fauntleroy (d. 1644), of Crondall, Hampshire.
Wallace's Virginia Hist. Mag., July, 1891.

FEILD, MRS. MARGARET (dead in 1772); wife of Dr. John Feild, Prince George county, and daughter of John Shaw (dead in 1772), merchant, of Edinburgh.
Prince George Records.

FELGATE, WILLIAM (d. 1660), York county; was in 1649 "of the City of London, skinner."
V. M., II, 181, 182.

FELL, HENRY (b. 1600, d. in Virginia 1623); "of Christchurch in Oxford, student." (B. A. Christ Church, 1620, "of London, gent."—*Foster*.)
V. M., XIX, 132, 133.

FIELDING, AMBROSE (d. 1675), Northumberland county; brother of Edward and Richard Fielding, merchants, of Bristol, and of Dr. Robert Fielding, of Gloucester.

V. M., XI, 453-456; XII, 99-101.

FILLBRIGGE, JOHN (in Virginia 1638, &c.) ; brother of Robert Fillbrigge, citizen and scrivenor, of London.

V. M., XII, 174.

FILMER, HENRY (in Virginia 1642, &c.), James City and Warwick counties; son of Sir Edward Filmer, of East Sutton, Kent, and his wife Elizabeth, daughter of Richard Argall, and sister of Samuel Argall, Governor of Virginia.

V. M., XV, 181, 182.   Berry's Kentish Genealogies.

FINCH, HENRY (in Virginia 1630, &c.) ; son of Sir Henry Finch, and brother of Sir John Finch, Speaker of the House of Commons, 1628-29.

V. M., VII, 384; XVII, 10.

FITZGEFFREY, GEORGE (in Virginia 1623), "of Howton Conquest in Bedfordshire, gent."

V. M., XIX, 133.

FITZGEFFREY, WILLIAM (in Virginia 1623), James City county; "of Staple Inn, gent."

V. M., XIX, 132, 133.

FITZHUGH, WILLIAM (1651-1701), Stafford county; son of Henry Fitzhugh, of the town of Bedford.

V. M., I, 413, 415; II, 277-278.

FLEET, HENRY (1600-1661), Lancaster county; son of William Fleet, gent., of Chartham, Kent, and his wife Deborah, daughter of Charles Scott, of Scottshall, Kent.

V. M., II, 71; V, 253, &c.

FLEETWOOD, EDWARD, gent. (d. 1609), went to Virginia 1609; son of Sir William Fleetwood, Recorder of London, and brother of Sir William Fleetwood, of Great Missendon, Bucks.

V. M., XIII, 405.

FLEMING, DANIEL (d. 1754), Louisa county; in his will he names his wife, then with him in Virginia, and children he had left in Lancashire.

Louisa County Records.

FLETCHER, GEORGE (in Virginia 1652, &c.), Northumberland county; brother of James Fletcher, gent., of Eltham, Kent. In 1647 George Fletcher was "of London, merchant."

Northampton Records. Hening, I, 374.

FLOURNOY, JACOB (1663-   ), Williamsburg; son of Jacques Flournoy, of Geneva, Switzerland, and uncle of John James Flournoy, of Virginia.

V. M., II, 85-87.

FLOURNOY, JOHN JAMES (1686-1740), Henrico county; son of Jacques Flournoy, of Geneva, Switzerland.

V. M., II, 83-84.

FONTAINE, JAMES (in Virginia 1717, &c.); son of Rev. James Fontaine, who was born at Jenouelle, France, and grandson of Rev. James Fontaine, pastor of Vaux and Royan.

Huguenot Emigration, 120, 121.

FONTAINE, REV. FRANCIS (1691-1749), York county; brother of Rev. James Fontaine, preceding.

Huguenot Emigration, 122.

FONTAINE, REV. PETER (1692-1757), Henrico and Charles City counties; brother of Rev. James Fontaine, preceding.

Huguenot Emigration, 122.

FOOTE, RICHARD (1632-1689, &c.), Stafford county; born at Cardenham, in the county of Cornwall; son of John Foote, gent.

V. M., VII, 73.

FORBY, BENJAMIN (in Virginia 1660, &c.), Princess Anne county; son of Felix Forby, of Norwich, hosier, who owned freeholds in Worstead and North Walsham, Norfolk.

V. M., XII, 398.

FORSE, JAMES (1706-1754), Northampton county; late of Devon.

W. M., XVI, 105.

FOUNTAINE, ROBERT (d. 1714), Princess Anne county. In will bequeaths "six messuages at Abingdon in Barkshire in Great Britain bequeathed to me in the will of my uncle, John Fountaine, and three messuages due me after the death of my Aunt Margaret Fountaine."

Princess Anne County Records.

FOWKE, GERRARD (d. 1669), Westmoreland county; son of Roger Fowke, of Gunston Hall, Staffordshire.

Hayden, 154-156, 744.

FOWKE, THOMAS (d. 1663), James City and Westmoreland counties; brother of Gerrard Fowke, preceding.

Hayden, 155.

FOXHALL, JOHN (d. 1704), Westmoreland county; left real and personal estate at Bromingham (Birmingham), Warwickshire.

V. M., XV, 301.

FREEMAN, HENRY, SR. (d. shortly before 1687), York county; formerly a mercer of Chipping Norton, Oxfordshire.

W. M., II, 164, 165.

FRY, JOSHUA (1700-1754), Essex county; son of Joseph Fry, "pleb.," of Crewkerne, Somerset.

W. M., II, 150. Foster's Oxford Matriculations.

GARLICK, SAMUEL (d. 1772), King and Queen county. His mother, at the date of his will, was Mrs. Hannah Garlick, of Bristol.

W. M., XVI, 101.

GERRARD, THOMAS (d. 1673), Westmoreland county; emigrated from England to Maryland; but removed to Virginia, where he died. In his will he gives to his son Justinian his right to any land in England. Justinian Gerrard was J. P. for

36

Westmoreland 1668, but removed to Maryland, where he died. In his will, dated 1682, he bequeathed lands in Lancashire.

Westmoreland County Records. Maryland Calendar of Wills, II, 40. Hayden's Virginia Genealogies, 490.

GILL, ALEXANDER (in Virginia 1623), Mulberry Island; "of Maldon in Bedfordshire."
V. M., XIX, 133, 134.

GLASSELL, JOHN (1734-1806), Fredericksburg; son of Robert Glassell, of Torthorwald, Dumfrieshire, Scotland.
Hayden, 4.

GLASSELL, ANDREW (1738-1827), Culpeper county; brother of John Glassell, preceding.
Hayden, 5.

GODDARD, ANTHONY (in Virginia 1663, d. 1663); formerly of Suringden, Wiltshire.
Maryland Calendar of Wills, I, 24.

GODSELL, JOHN (d. 1678), Lancaster county. His daughter lived at Charleville, Ireland.
Lancaster Records.

GOODE, JOHN (in Virginia 1678, &c.); brother of Rev. Marmaduke Goode, of Ufton, Berkshire.
W. G., 26.

GOODRICH, THOMAS (d. 1703), Essex county; son of Joseph Goodrich; his "uncle on the mother's side and next of kin," was Sir Abstroupus Danby, of Masham, Yorkshire.
V. M., XX, 93, 94.

GOOKIN, DANIEL (in Virginia 1621, &c.); of "Mary's Mount," near Newport News; formerly of Cargoline, Cork, Ireland; son of John Gookin, of Ripple Court, Kent.
V. M., VI, 71.

GORDON, GEORGE (d. 1786), Westmoreland county; bequeathed lands at Sheepbridge, Clogheramer, Lisduff, Carmern and Daryoghly, all in County Down, Ireland.
Westmoreland Records.

GORDON, JAMES (1714-1768), Lancaster county; son of James Gordon, gent., "of Sheepbridge and Lisduff, in the Lordship of Newry, County Down, Ireland."
W. M., XII, 11. Hayden, 248.

GORDON, JOHN (in Virginia 1738, &c.), Middlesex county; brother of James Gordon, preceding.
W. M., XII, 11. Hayden, 251, 252.

GORDON, REV. JOHN (d. about 1705), James City county; son of Patrick Gordon, Regent of King's College, Aberdeen.
Hayden, 617, 618.

GORDON, SAMUEL (1717-1771), Petersburg; son of David Gordon, Esq., of Craig, in the Stewartry of Kirkcudbright, Scotland.
W. M., VI, 22.

GORSUCH, REV. JOHN (d. about 1657), Lancaster county; formerly Rector of Walkholme, Hertfordshire; married Ann, daughter of Sir William Lovelace of Kent, and sister of Richard Lovelace, the poet.
V. M., III, 83.

GOSNOLD, ANTHONY (in Virginia 1615, &c.); grandson of Robert Gosnold, Esq., of Earleshall, Suffolk.
V. M., XIV, 87.

GOSNOLD, THOMAS (in Virginia 1702, &c.); son of Rebecca Gosnold, widow, of St. Martin's in the Fields, London, and nephew of David Ramage.
N. E. H. & G. Reg., Vol. 57, p. 95.

GOWTON, JOHN (in Virginia 1623); "of Harfield in Surrey, gent."
V. M., XIX, 133.

GRAHAM, JOHN (1711-1787), Prince William county; son of John Graham, Esq., of Wackinston, Perthshire, Scotland, and his wife Margaret, daughter of John Graham, Esq., of Killearn.
Hayden, 162.

GRAY, JOHN (1769-   ), Caroline county; son of William Gray (d. 1777), of Garlcraig, Scotland.

V. M., XI, 210.

GRAYSON, THOMAS (living in Virginia 1754, &c.), Spotsylvania county, in 1753; was "late of Deal in Kent, Eng,." though son of John Grayson, of Lancaster county, Va.

"Spotsylvania Records," p. 193.

GREENHOW, JOHN (1724-1787), Williamsburg; born at Staunton, near Kendal, Westmoreland; son of Robert and Ann (Dodgson) Greenhow, of High House, Staunton, near Kendal.

Va. Hist. Col., VI, 77. W. M., XVII, 273, 274.

GRENDON, THOMAS (d. 1685), Charles City county; grandson of Thomas Grendon, citizen and draper, of London (who d. 1678).

W. G., 429. V. M., XIV, 207.

GRIFFIN, LADY CHRISTINA (d. 1807), Williamsburg; wife of Judge Cyrus Griffin, and daughter of John Stuart, 6th Earl of Traquair.

V. M., I, 256, 467.

GRIFFIN, SAMUEL (d. 1703), Northumberland county; brother of David Griffin, citizen and tallow-chandler, of Bassinghall street, London. Samuel Griffin also owned property in Gloucestershire.

GRINLEY, JAMES (1743-1763), Williamsburg; son of Alexander Grinley, of Dunbar, Scotland.

Va. Hist. Col., XI, 71.

GROVE, JOHN, in Surry county 1668-69, &c.; in 1656 "of Bristol, merchant." He died in 1673.

Surry County Records.

GRYMES, WILLIAM (in Virginia 1694, &c.); son of Sir Thomas Grymes, of Peckham.

Richmond *Critic,* October 12, 1889.

GWYN, DAVID (d. 1704), Richmond county; had a sister Elizabeth, wife of Mr. Benjamin Gwyn, of Bristol, and a brother Edward Gwyn, clerk, in Wales. Left to his sister Mary all of his real estate in Wales lying in and about Harford West.
W. M., XVII, 83.

HACKE, DR. GEORGE (in Virginia 1663, &c.); Northampton county; born in Cologne in the Palatinate.
V. M., V, 256, &c.

HACKER, JOHN (in Virginia 1653, &c.); son of John Hacker, of Stepney, Middlesex, and nephew of Thomas Hacker, of Penzance, Cornwall.
W. G., 878.

HALLAM, ROBERT (1602-1637), Charles City county; brother of William Hallam, of Burnham, Essex.
W. M., VIII, 237-245. V. M., XIII, 55.

HALLAM, THOMAS (in Virginia 1656, &c.), Charles City county; son of Thomas Hallam of Essex (dead in 1656).
W. M., VIII, 243, 244.

HALLOWS, JOHN (in Virginia 1655, &c.), Westmoreland county, "late of Rochdale, in the county of Lancaster"; born about 1615. In 1732 his heir, Samuel Hallows, Esq., lived at Ashwick, Lancashire. He was a descendant of Samuel Hallows, of England, elder brother of John Hallows.
Westmoreland Records. Barton's Colonial Reports, II, B, 26.

HAMOR, RALPH, JR. (d. 1626); son of Ralph Hamor, citizen and merchant-tailor, of London.
W. G., 1000, 1012. V. M., I, 86.

HAMOR, THOMAS (in Virginia 1622, &c.); brother of Ralph Hamor, Jr., preceding.
W. G., 1000, 1012. V. M., I, 86.

HAMPTON, WILLIAM (in Virginia 1627, &c.); brother of Lawrence Hampton, of London, tailor.
W. G., 876.

HANDFORD, TOBIAS (d. 1677), Gloucester county; son of Hugh Handford, of London. John Handford, of Ludlow, Esq., by his will, dated 1669, left his manor of Shobden, Herefordshire, and other estates, in case of the death of his son John without issue, to the above Tobias Handford, of Virginia, with a farther reversion to Walter Handford, of Wallashall, Worcestershire.

V. M., XIII, 199-200.

HARECOURT, WILLIAM (in Virginia 1674, &c.), Lower Norfolk county; was dead in 1695, and his daughters and co-heiresses were Hannah, wife of William Hill, of Rockingham, Kent, and the wife of Henry Foster, of London.

Lower Norfolk Records.

HARMAR, CHARLES (d. about 1644), Northampton county; brother of Dr. John Harmar, Greek Professor at Oxford.

V. M., III, 274.

HARMAR, JOHN (in Virginia 1652, &c.); son of Dr. John Harmar, "Greek Reader in the University of Oxford."

V. M., III, 274.

HARRIS, JOHN (d. 1719), Northumberland county; son of Joseph Harris, and nephew of William Harris, of Haynie, in the parish of Stowford, Devon; mentions in his will (1718) a legacy from his uncle, then in the hands of Christopher Harris, Esq., of Padstow, Devon.

Northumberland Records.

HARRISON, BURR (in Virginia 1665, &c.), Stafford county; "baptized in the parish of St. Margaret's, Westminster, 28th December, 1637; son of Cuthbert Harrison."

Hayden, 512.

HARRISON, GEORGE (d. 1624); brother of Sir John Harrison, of Aldcliffe Hall, Lancashire.

Brown's Genesis, II, 913, 914.

HART, JOSYAS (in Virginia 1623), "of London, haberdasher."

V. M., XIX, 133.

HARVIE, JOHN (1706-1767), Albemarle county; born at Gargrannock, Scotland.
Va. Hist. Col., VI, 83.

HARWOOD, ARTHUR (d. 1642), formerly of the parish of St. Peter ad Vincula, London.
Mathews' Probate Acts.

HASSETT, SAMUEL (in Virginia before 1669), Isle of Wight county; brother of John Hassett, of Bristol, goldsmith.
W. M., VII, 227.

HAWKER, EDWARD (in Virginia 1657, &c.); brother of George Hawker, combmaker, of London.
V. M., XIII, 307.

HAWLEY, JEROME (in Virginia 1638, &c.); brother of James Hawley, of Brentford, Middlesex.
Neill's Virginia Carolorum, 142.

HAY, ALIAS GRAY, JOHN (d. 1709), Middlesex county; son of Dr. Gray, of Kendal and Whitehaven.
V. M., II, 45.

HAY, WILLIAM (1748-1825), Williamsburg; son of James Hay, and Helena Rankin his wife, of Kilsyth, Sterlingshire, Scotland.
W. M., XV, 85.

HAY, JOHN (in Virginia 1768, &c.), Southampton county; brother of William Hay, preceding.
W. M., XV, 85.

HAY, PETER (in Virginia 1768, &c.), Southampton county; brother of William Hay, preceding.
W. M., XV, 85.

HAYNES, HERBERT (d. 1737), Gloucester county; at time of death of St. Peter's, Cornhill, London. In will (1737) speaks of his rents in and about London. Son of Thomas Haynes, of Gloucester county, Va.
V. M., XV, 427.

HAYNES, THOMAS (d. 1679), Northumberland county; by will gave his brother, William Haynes, all his estate in houses, &c., in England, "which may be known by my father's will." Northumberland Records.

HAYWARD, SAMUEL (in Virginia 1687, &c.), Westmoreland county; son of Nicholas Hayward, grocer, of London.
W. M., XI, 169, 170.

HAZLEWOOD, GEORGE (in Virginia 1683, &c.), Middlesex county; son of John Hazlewood, of the parish of White Chapel, London. In 1693 his mother is referred to as "Madam Elizabeth Hazlewood at her house in Chamber street, Goodman's Fields, London."
Middlesex Records.

HENDERSON, ALEXANDER (d. 1815), came to Prince William county, Va., 1756; son of Rev. Richard Henderson, A. M., of Glasgow University, forty-eight years minister of Blantyre parish, Scotland, and his wife Janet Cleland.
Richmond *Critic,* June 9, 1889.

HENDERSON, JAMES (1708-1804), Augusta county; son of William Henderson, gent., of Fifeshire, Scotland, who married, on February 7, 1705, Margaret Bruce.
"Descendants of Lt. John Henderson."

HERBERT, JOHN (1658-1704), Prince George county; son of John Herbert, apothecary, and grandson of Richard Herbert, citizen and grocer, of London.
W. M., V, 230, 240; VIII, 147, 148.

HEYMAN, PETER (d. 1700), Elizabeth City county; grandson of Sir Peter Heyman, of Summerfield, in Kent.
V. M., XI, 158, 159.

HICKES, STEPHEN (d. shortly before 1640), Elizabeth City county; son of Michael Hickes and Judith his wife, of the town of Southampton. Stephen Hickes was baptized September 23, 1620, in the parish of St. Michael's, Southampton.
N. E. H. & G. Reg., Vol. 47, p. 353.

HIDE, JOHN (in Virginia 1635-37, &c.) ; son of Richard Hide, citizen and free-mason, of London.

V. M., XIX, 193.

HIGGINSON, ROBERT (d. 1649), York county; formerly a printer and painter-stainer, of London; son of Thomas and Anne Higginson, of Barkeswell, Warwickshire.

W. M., VI, 69.

HILL, EDWARD (in Virginia 1622, &c.), had, then, a brother, Mr. John Hill, mercer in Lombard street, and a father-in-law, Mr. Richard Boyle, in Blackfriars, London.

Brown's First Republic, p. 513.

HILL, ELIZABETH (in Virginia 1677, &c.) ; wife of Edward Hill, of "Shirley," Charles City county; daughter of Sir Edward Williams, of Brecknockshire, Wales.

V. M., III, 156-158; X, 107; XIV, 171.

HILL, HENRY (d. 1649), Northampton county; son of George Hill, of Tiverton, Devon.

Northampton Records.

HILL, JOHN (in Virginia 1647, &c.), Lower Norfolk county; formerly a bookbinder in the University of Oxford, and son of Stephen Hill, of Oxford, fletcher.

N. E. H. & G. Reg., Vol. 47, p. 53.

HILL, JOHN (d. 1720), of Virginia, but died at Newent, Gloucestershire.

V. M., XI, 74.

HODGE, THOMAS (d. 1784), King George county; in will, 1774, mentions his mother, then living at Tiverton, Devonshire.

King George Records.

HODGE, ROBERT (d. 1681), Lower Norfolk county; in 1670, was of Modbury, Devon.

Lower Norfolk Records.

HODGKIN, WILLIAM (came to Virginia 1659, d. 1673), old Rappahannock county; brother-in-law of Robert Peachey, of Mildenhall, Suffolk.

Rappahannock County Records.

HOGG, PETER (d. 1782), Augusta county; in Virginia 1756, &c.; son of James Hogg and brother of Walter Hogg, both of Edinburgh, Scotland.

Abstracts of Augusta Records, II, 220.

HOLECROFT, THOMAS (in Virginia 1610, &c.); son of Sir Thomas Holecroft, of Vale Royal, Cheshire.

Brown's Genesis, II, 924, 925.

HOLFORD, THOMAS (in Virginia 1668, &c.); son of John Holford, of Davenham, Cheshire, and his wife Jane, daughter of Thomas Mallory, Dean of Chester.

V. M., III, 328.

HOLLAND, SAMUEL (in Virginia 1638, &c.); son of Joseph Holland, citizen and clothworker, of London.

W. G., 9.

HOLLISTER, WILLIAM (d. 1680), Rappahannock county; brother of Thomas Hollister, of Temple Parish, Bristol.

Crozier's Virginia County Records, VI, 143.

HOLT, JAMES (in Virginia 1623), "of London, carpenter."

V. M., XIX, 134.

HONEYWOOD, SIR PHILIP (in Virginia 1649, &c.); son of Robert Honeywood, of Charing, Kent, and Mark's Hall, Essex.

Virginia Land Grants. Norwood's Voyage to Virginia. Note to Pepys.

HOOKE, FRANCIS (in Virginia 1635, &c.), Elizabeth City; son of John Hooke, Esq., of Bramshott, Southampton.

V. M., III, 23.

HOOPER, JOSEPH (in Virginia 1729, &c.); son of George Hooper, of Frome Selwood, Somerset.

Cabells and Their Kin, 21.

HOPE, GEORGE (1749-   ), Elizabeth City county; born in Cumberland.
W. M., VIII, 257.

HORNSBY, THOMAS (1702-1772), Williamsburg; born in Lincolnshire.
Va. Hist. Col., VI, 72.

HORSMANDEN, WARHAM (in Virginia 1657, &c.), Charles City county; returned to England and was of Lenham, Kent, and Purleigh, Essex; son of Rev. Daniel Horsmanden, Rector of Ulcombe, Kent, and his wife Ursula, daughter of Sir Warham St. Leger, of Ulcombe.
V. M., XV, 181, 182.

HORSENAIL, JAMES (d. 1731), Spotsylvania county; brother of Thomas Horsenail, of the parish of Nazing, Essex.
Spotsylvania Records.

HOSYER, EDWARD (in Virginia 1623), "of Ratcliffe, vintner."
V. M., XIX, 133, 134.

HOTHERSALL, THOMAS (came to Virginia 1621), "late zity-sone and grosser of London."
Brown's First Republic, p. 116.

HOWETT, JOHN (d. 1659), Elizabeth City county; brother of Thomas Howett, citizen and cooper, of London.
V. M., XIII, 55.

HUDSON, WILLIAM (died before 1716); brother of John Hudson, of Bristol, clothier (who d. 1725).
V. M., XV, 63.

HUME, FRANCIS (d. 1721), Spotsylvania county; brother of George Hume, of Wedderburn, Scotland (who d. 1720).
W. M., VI, 253; VIII, 84, &c. V. M., XX, 381, &c.

HUME, GEORGE (1697-1760), Spotsylvania and Culpeper counties, &c.; son of George Hume, of Wedderburn.
W. M., VI, 251, &c. V. M., 381, &c.

HUNT, REV. ROBERT (in Virginia 1607, &c.), of Kent, formerly Vicar of Reculver, Kent.
Campbell's History of Virginia.

HUNTER, WILLIAM, JR. (1731-1792) ; born at Galston, Scotland.
"Lodge of Washington," 95.

HUSSEY, GILES (d. 1668), Rappahannock county; son of James Hussey, Esq., of Blanford, Dorset, and brother of Thomas Hussey, of the same place, who was living in 1668.
Hayden, 298.

HUTT, DANIEL (d. 1674), Westmoreland county; formerly merchant of London, and at another time master of the ship *Mayflower*.
W. M., XV (Jan., 1907), 43, 49. Westmoreland Records.

IRBYE, WALTER (d. 1652), Northampton county; bequeathed tenements in Hoggstrap, Lincolnshire.
V. M., XVII, 67.

ISHAM, HENRY (1626-1676), in Henrico county 1657, &c.; son of William Isham (b. 1578, d. before 1631), and his wife Mary, daughter of William Brett, of Toddington, Bedfordshire, and grandson of Sir Euseby Isham, of Pytchley.
V. M., IV, 123. Victorian History of England, Northamptonshire.

IVESON, THOMAS (in Virginia 1700, &c.), Middlesex county; son of David Iveson, citizen and joiner, of London.
Middlesex Records.

JACKSON, REV. ANDREW (d. 1710), Lancaster county; brother of James Jackson, living in Potters' Fields near Belfast, Ireland.
Lancaster Records.

JACKSON, CHARLES (in Virginia 1667, &c.) ; son of Charles Jackson, of Darrington, Yorkshire.
Familiæ Minorum Gentium, III, 1070.

JACQUELIN, EDWARD (1668-1739), Jamestown; son of John and Elizabeth (Craddock) Jacquelin, of Kent.
W. M., IV, 49, 50.

JAUNCEY, WILLIAM (d. 1697), Lancaster county; had a brother John living at "Phen in Stratford, Buckinghamshire," and a sister Mary Boteler's children living at "Pharington, in Barkshire."
W. M., XI, 210.

JENIFER, DANIEL (in Virginia 1677, &c.), Northampton county; "brother" of John Steventon, merchant, of Creed Church Fryers, London.
Middlesex Records.

JENINGS, EDMUND (1659-1729), York county; son of Sir Edmund Jenings, of Ripon, Yorkshire.
V. M., XII, 307-310.

JERDONE, FRANCIS (1721-1771), Louisa county; son of John Jerdone, a magistrate of Jedburgh, Scotland.
W. M., VI, 37, 38.

JERMY, WILLIAM (d. 1666), Lower Norfolk county; in 1659 was "of Kettlebaston, Suffolk, gent."
N. E. H. & G. Reg., 1893, pp. 352, 355. Lower Norfolk Records.

JERVIS, FRANCIS (in Virginia 1661-81); son of Wm. Jervis (d. 1661), who owned a copyhold estate of £26 a year in Old Bradford, Middlesex, England.
Hist. MSS. Commission, House of Lords MSS., 1689-90, p. 362.

JOHNSON, LUKE (d. 1659); nephew of John Turton, of West Bromwich, County Stafford, gent.
V. M., XI, 366.

JOHNSON, RICHARD (d. 1698), King and Queen county. The account preserved in Virginia states that by his first marriage he had a daughter Judith, educated at a school in Lincoln, who m. Sir Hardoff Wastneys, about 1700. Burke's Extinct and Dormant Baronetage states that Sir Hardoff Wastneys, Bart., m. Judith, daughter and heir of Col. Richard Johnson, of Bilsby, Lincolnshire.

W. M., VI, 59, &c. Burke's Ex. and Dorm. Baronetage.

JOHNSON, MRS. SUSANNA (1664-1686), New Kent county (now King and Queen); wife of Col. Richard Johnson, and daughter of William Duncombe, Esq., of Holbeach, in the county of Lincoln.

Epitaph in King and Queen County.

JOHNSON, WILLIAM (in Virginia 1688, &c.), Middlesex county; of Norwich.

Ch. Ch., Middlesex, Parish Register.

JOHNSTON, ANDREW (1742-1785), Petersburg; "of Glasgow in Scotland."

W. M., IV, 232.

JONES, CADWALLADER (in Virginia 1681, &c.), Stafford county; son of Richard Jones, of London, merchant (lately deceased in 1681), who, together with John Jeffries, of London, owned the manor of Ley, in the parish of Beerfereis, Devon.

V. M., II, 31.

JONES, MRS. DOROTHY (1642-   ); wife of Roger Jones, of Virginia, and daughter of John Walker, Esq. (d. 1659), of Mansfield, Nottinghamshire.

Descendants of Capt. Roger Jones, pp. 34, 49, 196.

JONES, REV. EMANUEL (1668-1739), Gloucester county; son of John Jones, of Anglesea.

W. M., II, 150.

JONES, REV. ROWLAND (1644-1688), York county; son of Rowland Jones, of Kimbell, Bucks.

W. M., II, 150; V, 195. Foster's Oxford Matriculations.

JONES, WILLIAM (in Virginia 1640, &c.); born about 1614 at Ruthen, in the county of Denbigh.

Maryland Archives.

JONES, WILLIAM (in Virginia 1623), "in London, joyner."
V. M., XIX, 132.

JORDAN, MRS. ALICE (d. 1650), Surry county; wife of George
Jordan, and daughter of John Myles, gent., of Braunston, near
Hereford.
W. M., IV, 196; V, 6.

JOYE, WILLIAM (in Virginia 1619, &c.) ; son of Robert Joye,
and nephew of Thomas Stacie, gent., of Maidstone, Kent.
V. M., XIII, 405.

KAY, JAMES (died in 1677), Rappahannock county; "a Lancashire man."
W. M., VII, 115, 118.

KAY, WILLIAM (was dead in 1726), Rappahannock county;
"a Lancashire man."
W. M., VII, 118.

KELLOWAY, WILLIAM (b. about 1603, in Virginia 1623), "of
Porchmouth (Portsmouth), husbandman."
V. M., XIX, 133.

KELSALL, REV. ROGER (d. 1708), Norfolk county; refers in
his will to an estate left him by his father, Rev. Roger Kelsall,
"Minister of Royden, known by the name of Byers St. Mary's,
adjoining Colchester."
W. M., XX, 188. Abstracts of Norfolk County Wills, p. 195.

KELSICK, RICHARD (died about 1760), Norfolk Borough;
formerly of Whitehaven.
Lower Norfolk County, Va., Antiquary, I, 7.

KEMPE, WILLIAM (in Virginia 1623), "of Howes in Leicestershire, gent."
V. M., XIX, 132.

KENDALL, WILLIAM (d. 1686), Northampton county; legacies
to his brother John Kendall, "living about Brinton in Norfolk,"
and to brother Thomas Kendall, of Norwich.
Northampton Records.

KENNEDY, ALEXANDER (d. 1760), Elizabeth City county; bequests to Christ Church parish, Cork, Ireland; to the poor of that city, &c.

Elizabeth City Records.

KESTON, THOMAS (in Virginia 1667, &c.) ; brother of Francis Keston, of All Saints' Barking, London, who left a legacy to the poor of Great Bowden, Leicestershire.

V. M., XI, 309.

KINGSWELL, EDWARD, ESQ. (1578-1636), in Virginia 1633; in 1633 was of St. Sepulchres, London.

Chester's Faculty Office Marriage Licenses. V. M., XV, 297, &c.

KINGSWELL, JANE (b. about 1593), in Virginia 1633; wife of Edward Kingswell (marriage license February 27, 1632-3), and before widow of Sir William Clifton, of Little Gidding, Huntingdonshire. .

Chester's Faculty Office Marriage Licenses. V. M., XV, 297, &c.

KNIGHT, NATHANIEL, chirurgeon (d. 1677), Surry county; son of Samuel Knight, of Stroodwater, Gloucestershire.

Surry Records.

LANDON, THOMAS (d. 1701), Middlesex county; son of Silvanus Landon, of Crednall, or Credenhill, Herefordshire.

V. M., II, 430, 433. Keith's Ancestry of Benjamin Harrison.

LANGBORNE, WILLIAM (1723-1766), King William county; son of Robert Langborne, of Fetter Lane, London.

W. M., IV, 166.

LATHBURY, JOHN (d. 1655), formerly citizen and pewterer of London.

V. M., XII, 406.

LAWNE, CHRISTOPHER (d. 1620), Charles City; of Blanford, Dorset.

Lea's P. C. C. Abstracts, 1620.

LAWRENCE, REV. JOHN (d. 1684), Lower Norfolk county; baptized at Wormleyberry House, parish of Wormley, Herefordshire; son of John and Dorothy Lawrence. He bequeathed six tenements in Church Lane, in the parish of St. Giles in the Fields, London.

V. M., II, 176.

LAWSON, ANTHONY (d. 1701), Lower Norfolk county; was in 1669 a merchant of Londonderry, Ireland. In Virginia 1673, &c.

"Lower Norfolk county, Va., Antiquary," I, 47, 48.

LE BRETON, JOHN; in Northumberland county, Va., 1664, &c. Had a brother, Edward Le Breton, of the Island of Jersey.

Northumberland Records.

LEE, PETER (d. before 1688), Henrico county; brother of Richard Lee, of London, gent., who was alive 1686.

Henrico Records.

LEE, DR. WILLIAM (in Virginia 1660, &c.); brother of George Lee, citizen and grocer, of London.

LIGHTFOOT, PHILIP (d. 1708), York, &c., counties; son of John Lightfoot, Esq., of Gray's Inn.

W. M., II, 91-97; III, 104, &c.

LIGHTFOOT, JOHN (d. 1707), New Kent county; brother of Philip Lightfoot, preceding.

W. M., II, 204. V. M., VII, 397.

LINDSAY, REV. DAVID (1603-1667), Northumberland county; eldest son of Sir Hierome Lindsay, of The Mount, Lord Lyon King at Arms, Scotland.

V. M., XVIII, 90-92.

LINDSAY, JOHN (in Virginia about 1675), in 1682 was of Bradwinch, Devon.

Middlesex Records.

LISTER, THOMAS (1708-1740); son of James Lister, of Shibden Hall, Yorkshire.

W. M., III, 245, 246.

LISTER, WILLIAM (1712-1743); brother of Thomas Lister, preceding.
W. M., III, 245.

LITTLETON, NATHANIEL (d. 1654), Northampton county; son of Sir Edward Littleton, of Henley, Shropshire.
W. M., VIII, 230, 231; IX, 62. V. M., XVIII, 20.

LLOYD, CORNELIUS (in Virginia 1635, &c.), Lower Norfolk county; formerly "of London, merchant."
N. E. H. & G. Reg., Vol. 47, p. 69.

LLOYD, JOHN (in Virginia 1692, &c.), Rappahannock and Richmond counties; removed to England in 1694, was at one time of the city of Chester, and in 1716 described as "John Lloyd, of Bacheckrick, County of Denbigh, Esq."
V. M., V, 160-161. N. E. H. & G. Reg., Vol. 59, p. 219.

LLOYD, THOMAS (d. 1699), Richmond county; brother of John Lloyd, preceding.
V. M., V, 160-161. Richmond County Records. N. E. H. & G. Reg., Vol. 59, p. 219.

LLOYD, WILLIAM (in Virginia 1667, &c.); (father of John and Thomas Lloyd).
W. M., XVII, 75.

LLUELLIN, DANIEL (d. 1664), Charles City county; formerly of Chelmsford, Essex.
V. M., XIII, 53, &c.

LOCKEY, EDWARD (d. 1667), York county; brother of John Lockey, merchant, of London.
W. M., III, 278.

LOCKLEY, WILLIAM (d. 1745), owned freeholds in "poor Jury Lane *als* Crutched Fryars, parish St. Catherine Cree Church and Christ Church, London"; his mother Jane, was, in 1738, wife of Joseph Studley, of Nicholas Lane, London, gent.

LOMAX, JOHN (1674-1729), Essex and Caroline counties; son of Rev. John Lomax, M. A., of Emanuel College, Cambridge;

Rector of Wooler, Northumberland, who was evicted in 1662, and died at North Shields, 1674.

Lomax Bible Record, &c.

LOVELACE, FRANCIS (in Virginia 1651, &c.); son of Sir William Lovelace, of Woolwich, Kent, and brother of Richard Lovelace, the poet; was afterwards Governor of New York.

V. M., XVII, 287.

LOWE, MICAJAH, merchant (d. 1704), Charles City county, but died at Carshaulton, Surrey, England; nephew of Micajah Perry, merchant, of London.

V. M., XI, 310.

LOWNDS, JOHN (in Virginia 1654, &c.), Lower Norfolk county; brother of Nathaniel Lownds, of London, merchant. John Lownds was entitled to certain lands, &c., at Salford, in the county of Lancaster, formerly the property of Edmund Knott, whose right heir he was.

Lower Norfolk Records.

LUDLOW, FRANCIS (d. about 1670), son of Gabriel Ludlow; had a brother, Mr. John Ludlow, who died about the same time. Col. John Carter was administrator of Francis Ludlow.

Lancaster Records. W. G., 172, 276.

LUDLOW, GEORGE (1596-1656), York county; son of Thomas Ludlow, Esq., of Dinton, Wiltshire.

W. G., 172, 276. W. M., II, 4, 5.

LUDLOW, THOMAS (1624-1660), York county; son of Gabriel Ludlow, Barrister at Law.

W. G., 172, 276. W. M., II, 4, 5.

LUDWELL, THOMAS (d. 1698), James City county; son of Thomas Ludwell, of Bruton, Somerset, mercer, and his wife Jane, daughter of James Cottington, of Discoe, in the parish of Bruton, gent., and niece of Francis, Lord Cottington.

W. M., I, 110.

LUDWELL, PHILIP (in Virginia 1675, &c.), James City county; brother of Thomas Ludwell, preceding.

LUKE, GEORGE (in Virginia 1690, &c.), Westmoreland county; son of Oliver Luke, Esq., of Woodend, Bedfordshire.
V. M., III, 167, 168.

LUNSFORD, SIR THOMAS (1610-1653), James City county; son of Thomas Lunsford, Esq., of Lunsford and Wilegh, Sussex, and his wife Katherine, daughter of Sir Thomas Fludd, Treasurer of War to Queen Elizabeth.
V. M., XVII, 26-33.

LUPO, PHILIP (d. 1670), Isle of Wight county; son of Philip Lupo, goldsmith, of London.
Isle of Wight Records.

LYDE, CORNELIUS (d. 1737), King William county; son of Lyonel Lyde, Esq., Mayor of Bristol (who d. 1744).
W. M., VII, 138. Burke's Extinct and Dormant Baronetage.

LYDE, STEPHEN (1681-1715), Essex county; son of Cornelius Lyde, Esq., of Staunton Wick, Somerset.
Essex Records. Burke's Extinct and Dormant Baronetage.

LYNCH, HEAD (baptized November 12, 1712, at Staple, Kent), Caroline county, 1739, &c.; son of John Lynch, Esq., of Groves in Staple, Kent, and his wife Sarah, daughter of Francis Head, Esq., of Rochester, Kent.
Pedigrees from the Visitation of Kent, 1663-68, pp. 46, 49. Berry's Kentish Pedigrees. V. M., XIV, 341; XV, 11, 118.

LYNN, DR. WILLIAM (d. 1758), Spotsylvania county; brother of Charles and Audley Lynn, of Ireland; kinsman of Moses Lynn in Strabane and Lieutenant Mathew Lynn, near Londonderry, Ireland.
Spotsylvania Records.

McADAM, JOSEPH (in Virginia 1769, &c.), Northumberland county; married at Govan, Scotland, to Janet Muir.

McPHERSON, ARCHIBALD (1705-1749), Fredericksburg; "born in the county of Murray, in North Briton."
W. M., X, 108.

MACKIE, JOHN (1731-1750), Petersburg; son of Patrick Mackie, merchant, and provost of Wigton, Scotland.

W. M., V, 237.

MACKIE, REV. JOSIAS (d. 1716), Norfolk county; son of Patrick Mackie, of St. Johnstone, county of Donegal, Ireland.

W. M., VII, 358, 359.

McRAE, REV. CHRISTOPHER (1733-1808), in Virginia before 1765; Surry and Cumberland counties; entered Marischal College, Aberdeen, in 1749, and was graduated M. A. in 1753; son of Christopher McRae, of Urquhart, Rosshire.

Anderson's Records of Marischal College, Vol. II, p. 320. Meade's Old Churches and Families of Virginia, II, 36, 37.

MADDISON, THOMAS (d. 1674), Rappahannock county; had in 1674 a brother, Leonard Maddison, living in England.

Crozier's "Virginia County Records," VI, 10.

MALLORY, REV. PHILIP (1617-1661), York county; son of Thomas Mallory, D. D., Dean of Chester, and grandson of Sir William Mallory, of Studley, Yorkshire.

V. M., XII, 398, 399; XIV, 102.

MALLORY, ROGER (in Virginia 1660, &c.), King and Queen county; son of Thomas Mallory, D. D., Rector of Eccleston, Lancashire, and grandson of Thomas Mallory, Dean of Chester.

V. M., XII, 401; XV, 106.

MALLORY, THOMAS (in Virginia 1660, &c.); brother of Roger Mallory, preceding.

V. M., XII, 401; XV, 106.

MANFIELD, GEORGE (d. 1670), Surry county; nephew of John Beale, citizen and grocer, of London.

V. M., XI, 311.

MAREEN (MARIN), MRS. SUSAN (in Virginia 1707, &c.), Henrico county; sister of Wiltshire Reeve, of Hubbards Hall in the parish of Harlow, Essex, gent., who in his will (1707) leaves her all his plantation, &c., on or near James River in Virginia. A Wiltshire Mairin lived in Henrico in 1746.

N. Y. B. and G. Record, XLIII, 69, 70. Stith's History of Virginia.

MARSHALL, ABRAHAM (d. 1709), Richmond county; had a brother John Marshall, "of Bradfield in Barkshire."
Richmond County Records.

MARTIN, DAVID (d. 1767), Amherst county; son of Mrs. Jennet Martin of the townland of Curryreagh, parish of Cardonnel, county Down, Ireland.
Amherst County Records.

MARTIN, HENRY, "went to Virginia many years ago" (statement in will 1786); brother of Sparks Martin, Esq., of Withy Bush House, county Pembroke, who d. 1787.
V. M., XIII, 197.

MARTIN, JOHN, "went to Virginia many years ago"; brother of Henry Martin, preceding.
V. M., XIII, 197-199.

MARTIN, JOHN (in Virginia 1752, &c.), King and Queen and Caroline counties. Removed to Dublin where he died in 1760. Two of his daughters married Viscount Clifden and Viscount Perry. He was brother of George Martin, Esq., of Dublin, Doctor of Physic, who died 1755.
Caroline County Records, V. M., XIII, 197-199; XXI, 249, 372.

MARTIN, JOHN (in Virginia 1607, &c.); son of Sir Richard Martin, goldsmith, of London.
Brown's Genesis, II, 943-944.

MARTIN, RALPH (in Virginia 1623), "of Bachain, Somersetshire, husbandman."
V. M., XIX, 134.

MATTHEWS, LUKE (in Virginia 1694, &c.); formerly a tailor in the city of Hereford.
V. M., IV, 365; VI, 408, 409.

MAURY, MRS. ANN (1690-   ), Henrico county; wife of Matthew Maury, and sister of Rev. James Fontaine (above).
Huguenot Emigration, 122.

MAURY, MATTHEW (d. 1752), Henrico county; of Castle Mauron, Gascony, France.
Huguenot Emigration, 122.

MAXWELL, JAMES (d. 1795), Norfolk Borough; of Northumberland.
Lower Norfolk county, Va., Antiquary, II, 56, &c.

MAYO, WILLIAM (1684-1744), Goochland county; son of Joseph Mayo and Elizabeth (Hooper) Mayo, of Frome Selwood, Somerset.
Richmond *Standard,* July, 1880. Cabells and Their Kin.

MAYO, JOSEPH (1692-   ), Henrico county; brother of William Mayo, preceding.
Richmond *Standard,* July 17, 1880. Cabells and Their Kin.

MEADE, MRS. SUSANNAH, wife of David Meade, of Nansemond county; (married 1729-30), and daughter of Sir Richard Everard, Bart., of Much Waltham, Essex.
W. M., XIII, 39, 40.

MERCER, BURRADINE (in Virginia 1654, &c.); brother of William Mercer, citizen and haberdasher, of London.
V. M., XIV, 425.

MERCER, JAMES (d. 1759), Stafford county; brother of John Mercer (next).
V. M., XIV, 233, 234.

MERCER, JOHN (1704-1768), Stafford county; born in Church street, Dublin, Ireland; son of John and Grace (Fenton) Mercer of that city.
V. M., XIV, 232-234.

MERCER, HUGH (1726-1777), Fredericksburg (but settled first in Pennsylvania); son of Rev. William Mercer, minister of

Pittsligo, Aberdeenshire, and his wife Ann, daughter of Sir Robert Munro, of Foulis.

Goolrick's Life of General Hugh Mercer, pp. 12, 13, 105.

METCALFE, RICHARD (in Virginia 1688, &c.); son of Gilbert Metcalfe, merchant, of London, and Jane, his wife.

W. M., V, 10-12.

METCALFE, THOMAS (1734-   ), King and Queen county; son of Samuel Metcalfe, grocer, of Nantwich, Chesire.

W. M., V, 13, 14.

MICHAUX, ABRAHAM (d. 1717), Henrico county; born at Sedan, in France.

Henrico Records.

MICHELSON, JOHN (d. 1750), Yorktown?; son of James Michelson, jeweller, in Edinburgh.

Will, P. C. C., Glazier 227.

MIDDLETON, ROBERT (d. 1627); brother of William Middleton, of Hampton, Yorkshire.

W. G., 1022.

MILL, JAMES (in Virginia 1752, &c., d. 1765), King William county; son of James Mill, of Penlochton, Shire of Angus, Scotland.

W. M., XX, 208.

MILLS, CHARLES (d. before 1783), Hanover county; owned a farm called Goringe in the parish of Thundersley, North Ben Fleet, Essex, and a farm called Sayers, Sawyers or Grey House in the same parish and county; both held of the manor of Eastwood or Eastonbury, Essex, which were sold by his heirs in 1783.

Hanover County Records.

MOLESWORTH, GUY (in Virginia 1651, &c.); son of William Molesworth, Esq., and grandson of Anthony Molesworth, Esq., of Fotheringay, Northamptonshire.

Burke's Peerage. Minutes of Virginia Council.

MONTAGUE, PETER (1603-1659), Lancaster county; son of Peter and Eleanor Montague, of Boveny, parish of Burnham, Bucks.

Montague Genealogy, pp. 30, 31 and chart.

MOON, JOHN (d. 1655), Isle of Wight county; born at Berry, near Gosport, in the parish of Stoak in Hampshire; bequeathed lands at Berry and Alverstoak, near Gosport and Plymouth.

W. M., VII, 222.

MORYSON, CHARLES (d. 1688), Elizabeth City county; son of Richard Moryson and Winifred his wife, and grandson of Sir Richard Moryson, of Tooley Park, Leicestershire.

V. M., II, 384, 385. W. M., IX, 92-94, 119-121, 122.

MORRISON, CHARLES (in Virginia about 1760); formerly a surgeon of Greenock, Scotland.

V. M., XXII, 201.

MORYSON, FRANCIS (in Virginia 1649, &c.), Elizabeth City county and Jamestown; son of Sir Richard Moryson, of Tooley Park, Leicestershire.

V. M., II, 384, 385. W. M., IX, 119, &c.

MORYSON, RICHARD (d. 1646), Elizabeth City county; brother of Francis Moryson, preceding.

V. M., II, 383-385.

MORYSON, ROBERT (d. 1647), Elizabeth City county; brother of Francis Moryson, preceding.

V. M., II, 383-385. W. M., IX, 122-123.

MOSELEY, WILLIAM (d. 1655), Lower Norfolk county; formerly of Rotterdam, merchant; but of English birth or descent. Lower Norfolk Records.

MOULLE, WILLIAM (in Virginia 1655, &c.), Northampton county; brother of Francis Moulle, of Ashby Folwell in the county of Leicester, gent. (alive 1656).

Northampton Records.

MOULSON, FULKE (in Virginia 1674, &c.); brother of Peter Moulson, of London, gent., who mentions in his will his nephew, Peter Moulson, of Warton, *als* Wavlston, and states that he (the testator) was born in the parish of Wharton, Cheshire.

V. M., XIII, 403, 404.

MOUNTJOY, EDWARD (in Virginia 1695, &c.), Westmoreland county; brother of Thomas Mountjoy, of Bristol, merchant.

V. M., XVI, 291.

MOYE, JOHN (d. 1645), Lower Norfolk county; married a daughter of Richard Wheeler, citizen and innholder, of London.

V. M., XIII, 407. N. Y. Gen. & Biog. Record, XL, 86.

MUNFORD, WILLIAM (in Virginia 1668, &c.), York county. In 1657 there is a power of attorney (rec. in York county) from Sarah Harrison, of London, to Wm. Munford, of same, tobacconist; and a power of attorney, dated 1668, from Ann, widow of Augustine Munford, citizen and grocer of London, and John Munford, citizen and grocer of London, to Wm. Munford, of York county, Va. Whether Wm. Munford was ancestor of later families of the name is not known.

York County Records.

MUSCO, SALVATOR (b. 1704, d. 1741), Essex; in his will states that his sister, Mrs. Jane Collingwood, of Great Britain, had, in her will dated September 30, 1730, left him £400.

Essex Records.

MUSGRAVE, MICHAEL (d. 1697), Middlesex county; brother of Thomas Musgrave, Rector of Woolbeding, Essex, and Prebendary of Chichester (who d. 1725).

V. M., XII, 207, 208; XIV, 93, 94.

NASH, JOHN (d. 1776), Henrico and Prince Edward counties; son of Abner Nash, of Tenby, in South Wales.

Henrico and Prince Edward Records.

NASH, THOMAS (d. 1737), Henrico county; brother of John Nash, preceding.

Henrico Records.

NEDHAM, JAMES (d. 1677); brother of George Nedham, Esq., and son of Barbara Nedham, deceased.

V. M., XI, 75.

NEEDLER, BENJAMIN (d. 1741), King and Queen county; son of Culverwell Needler, clerk assistant to the House of Commons.

V. M., XIV, 26.

NELSON, NATHANIEL, merchant (d. before 1696), New Kent county; brother of Henry Nelson, of Penrith Cumberland, yeoman.

Middlesex Records.

NELSON, THOMAS (1677-1745), Yorktown; son of Hugh Nelson, gent., and Sarah his wife, of Penrith.

V. M., XIII, 402, 403.

NEWCE, SIR WILLIAM (in Virginia 1622); formerly of Bandon, Cork, Ireland, but of English birth.

Neill's Virginia Carolorum, 81, 82.

NEWCE, THOMAS (in Virginia 1622, &c.), brother of Sir William Newce, preceding.

Neill's Virginia Carolorum.

NEWMAN, EDWARD (in Virginia 1672, &c.), nephew of Zacharie Irish, one of the petty canons of the chapel of Windsor Castle.

W. G., 1017.

NEWTON, JOHN (d. 1697), Westmoreland county; had lived at Anlaby, Yorkshire; eldest son of Thomas Newton, of Hull. John Newton bequeathed lands at Carlton and Camelsforth, Yorkshire, and the house in Hull "which was my father's."

V. M., I, 69. Westmoreland Records.

NICHOLSON, JAMES (d. 1686), Middlesex county; of Ixby, Cumberland.

Ch. Ch., Middlesex, Parish Register.

Nicolls, Richard, tailor (in Virginia 1650, &c.), Lower Norfolk county; son of Henry Nicolls, innholder, dwelling at the sign of the White Horse, Oxenbury, Huntingdonshire.

N. E. H. & G. Reg., Vol. 47, p. 353.

Nicolson, James (1711-1773), Williamsburg; born at Inverness, Scotland.

Va. Hist. Col., XI, 73.

Nimmo, William (d. 1748), Williamsburg; brother of John Nimmo, of Blackridge, in the county of Linlithgow, Scotland.

W. M., V, 134-136.

Norton, John (1719-1777), York county; son of John Norton and his wife Susanna, daughter of Henry Hatley.

Norton Family Records.

Nourse, James (1731-1784); born at Weston-under-Penyard, Herefordshire, July 19, 1731; third son of John Nourse.; came to Virginia 1769.

V. M., VII, 199. Life of James Nourse. West Va. Hist. Mag., 1904, p. 284.

Noye, Philip (d. 1650); returned to England and at death was "of Burian now of St. Just, Cornwall," first cousin of Attorney-General William Noye.

V. M., XIV, 424, 425.

Oldis, William (in Virginia 1668, &c.), Isle of Wight county; brother of Valentine Oldis, citizen and apothecary, of London.

W. M., VII, 226.

Oliver, William (d. 1686), Middlesex county; of the Isle of Ely near Cambridge.

Ch. Ch., Middlesex, Parish Register.

Opie, Thomas, Jr. (d. 1702), Northumberland county; "of Bristol." (Epitaph.)

W. M., XI, 129.

OSWALD, HENRY, formerly chirurgeon, of Kirkaldie, Scotland (b. 1694, d. 1726), Essex county; in his will refers to his lands and houses in Scotland, particularly "the house where Provost Henry Oswald lived." He was son of Thomas Oswald, formerly "prefectus" (provost?) of Kirkaldie.

Essex Records. Richmond *Critic*, August 23, 1890.

OVERTON, MRS. ELIZABETH, wife of William Overton (b. 1628), King William county; daughter of Ann Waters, of St. Sepulchre's, London, widow (d. 1697).

V. M., XI, 305, 306.

OWEN, REV. G R O N O W Y (1722-1770), Williamsburg and Brunswick county; (famous Welsh poet); born at Llanfair Mathafan, Wales; son of Owen Gronowy.

W. M., IX, 152-154.

OXWICK, THOMAS, "of London, living some time in Virginia" (1646); son of Francis Oxwick, of London, merchant, and his wife Susan, daughter of Thomas Corbett, D. D., of Stanway, County Essex.

Genealogist (N. S.), XXIII, 122.

PACY, GEORGE (in Virginia 1623), "of London, grocer."
V. M., XIX, 134.

PAGE, JOHN (1627-1692), York county; son of Francis Page, gent., of Bedfont, Middlesex.

Page Family (1893), 9-40.

PAIN, ROBERT (d. 1717), Richmond county; made bequest to the poor of St. Sepulchre's parish, London, and to his wife's brother, Henry Williamson, in London.

W. M., XVII, 180.

PARKE, REV. H E N R Y (in Virginia 1653, &c.), Accomac county; in 1653 owned a tract of land in Accomac in partnership with George Parke, of Doncaster, merchant.

Accomac Records.

PARKE, MRS. REBECCA, wife of Daniel Parke, of York county (d. 1672), daughter of George Evelyn and granddaughter of Robert Evelyn, of Long Ditton, Surrey.

V. M., IX, 173; XIV, 174, 175.

PARKER, GEORGE (in Virginia before 1673); son of James Parker, and grandson of William Parker, Archdeacon of Cornwall, who lived at Trangoe, in the parish of Wartegin, Cornwall.

V. M., V, 442-444; XIX, 191, 192.

PARKER, JAMES (in Virginia 1687, &c.), New Kent county; of Southwell, Nottinghamshire.

Ch. Ch., Middlesex, Parish Register.

PARKER, PHILIP (in Virginia 1656, &c.), Northampton county; brother of Thomas Parker, citizen and draper, of London.

Northampton Records.

PARKER, DR. RICHARD (in Virginia before 1673); brother of George Parker, preceding.

V. M., V, 443.

PARKER, ROBERT (d. 1673), Northampton county; was of Bosham, Sussex, at time of death; bequeathed in will his land at Bosham and Meadhurst; sold or leased about 1656 land called Coper's (or Soper's) Hall; states in will that his father and grandfather were buried in the Church of St. Lawrence, Southampton.

V. M., XVII, 65-67.

PARKER, WILLIAM (in Virginia 1765, &c., d. 1798), Spotsylvania county; in 1773 "Wm. Parker, gent., and his son Alexander Parker, Jr.," gave power of attorney to Hugh Houston to take action in regard to certain property in St. Michael's parish, Bristol.

"Spotsylvania Records" (N. Y., 1905), p. 308.

PAWLETT, THOMAS (1578-1644), Charles City county; son of Chidiock Pawlett, and grandson of William Pawlett, 1st Marquis of Winchester. Thomas Pawlett in his will mentions his brother Chidiock Pawlett, and leaves most of his estate to his brother, Sir John Pawlett, who, in 1665, was of Winchester.

W. M., IV, 151-153. Brown's Genesis, II, 962. Collins' Peerage.

PAYNE, NICHOLAS (in Virginia 1687, &c.), Middlesex county; of London.

Ch. Ch., Middlesex, Parish Register.

PEACHEY, SAMUEL (d. 1712), Richmond county; son of Robert Peachey and Anne (Hogskin) his wife, of Milden Hall, Suffolk.

W. M., III, 111-113.

PEALE, MALACHY (in Virginia 1674, &c.), Westmoreland county; in 1673 was of Exeter, Devon.

Westmoreland Records.

PEGDEN, JOHN (d. in Virginia 1623), James City; "of London, gent."

V. M., XIX, 133.

PERCY, GEORGE (1580-1632), 8th son of Henry, 8th Earl of Northumberland.

Brown's Genesis, II, 964.

PERIN, JOHN (in Virginia 1686, &c.), Middlesex county; of Sussex.

Ch. Ch., Middlesex, Parish Register.

PERRY, PETER (in Virginia 1685, &c.), York county; brother of Micajah Perry, merchant, of St. Catherine Cree, London.

W. M., XVII, 265.

PERRY, ROBERT (in Virginia 1652, &c.); son of Mrs. Flizabeth Perry, and nephew of Robert Perry, of Bristol, clerk.

V. M., XI, 363.

PETER, JOHN (d. 1763), Surry county; son of Thomas Peter, and brother of Alexander Peter, of Glasgow, Scotland.

PETER, WALTER (in Virginia 1763, &c.); brother of John Peter, preceding.
Surry Records.

PETTUS, THEODORE (in Virginia 1623); "of Norwich, gent."
V. M., XIX, 133.

PEYTON, ROBERT (1640-1694), Gloucester county; son of Thomas and Elizabeth (Yelverton) Peyton, of Rougham, Norfolk, and grandson of Sir Edward Peyton, Bart., of Isleham, Cambridgeshire.
Hayden's Virginia Genealogies, 461-468.

PEYTON, HENRY (1630-1659), Westmoreland county; son of Henry Peyton, Esq., of Lincoln's Inn (d. 1656), and brother of Sir Robert Peyton, Knt., of East Barnet (d. 1689).
Hayden's Virginia Genealogies, 490, &c.

PEYTON, VALENTINE (1627-1665), Westmoreland county; brother of Henry Peyton, preceding.
Hayden, 480-488.

PHILLIPS, JOHN (in Virginia 1704, &c.); uncle of Robert Phillips, of Bristol, mariner.
V. M., XIII, 308.

PIGHTLING, PHILIP (d. 1701), Princess Anne county; in will styled "of Horsted, son of John Pightling, gent.," and refers to the "great Bible" given him by his godfather, Col. Philip Harbord.
Princess Anne County Records.

PIGOT, JOHN (in Virginia 1654, &c.), Lower Norfolk county; formerly citizen and merchant tailor, of London.
N. E. H. & G. Reg., Vol. 47, p. 20.

PITT, ROBERT (d. 1714), Northampton county; bequeathed his rights in tenements, premises, &c., under the will of his mother, Mrs. Mary Pitt, of Bristol.
Northampton Records.

PLACE, ROWLAND (1642-1713), of Dimsdale, Yorkshire, Esq.
W. M., XV, 49.

PLATT, RANDOL, or RANDOLPH (d. about 1719), New Kent and Prince George counties; son of William Platt, of the parish of Prescott, town of Whiston, Lancashire.
Prince George Records.

PLEASANTS, JOHN (1645-1649), Henrico county; son of John Pleasants, of Norwich, worstead weaver.
V. M., XVII, 320.

PLOWDEN, SIR EDMUND (in Virginia 1641, &c., d. 1659), Elizabeth City and Northampton counties; son of Francis Plowden, of Plowden, Shropshire. He was in America 1641-48 for the purpose of establishing his colony on the Delaware, but was most of the time in Virginia.
Northampton County Records. N. Y. Gen. and Biog. Record, XL, 87, &c.

POINDEXTER (POINGDESTRE), GEORGE, York county, 1660, &c.; son of Thomas Poingdestre (b. 1581), Seigneur of the fief es Poingdestre, Island of Jersey.
V. M., XIX, 215-218.

PONSONBY, JOHN (in Virginia 1772, &c.), Dinwiddie county; son of John Ponsonby, of Whitehaven.
V. M., XXIII, 203.

POOLE, WILLIAM (in Virginia 1623); "of Preston in Andernesse in Lankeshire."
V. M., XIX, 132.

POPE, RICHARD (in Virginia 1690, &c.), Isle of Wight county; brother of John Pope, of the parish of Dawlish, mariner.
Isle of Wight Records.

POPELEY, RICHARD (in Virginia 1627, &c.), James City county; born in 1608 in the parish of Wolley, Yorkshire.
W. M., III, 169.

PORTEUS, EDWARD (d. 1700), Gloucester county; refers in will to his father's estate in Newbottle, Scotland.
V. M., XIII, 310, 311.

POULTER, THOMAS (in Virginia 1661, &c.); son of John Poulter, of Hitchen, Hertfordshire.
W. G., 67, 68.

POVALL, ROBERT (1650-1728), Henrico county; formerly of St. Martin's in the Fields, London.
Povall Bible Record.

POWELL, THOMAS (in Virginia 1695, &c.), Middlesex county; in 1695 styled "Thomas Powell the younger late of the City of Hereford."
Middlesex Records.

POWELL, PYTHOGORAS (in Virginia 1686, &c.), Middlesex county; of Catesby, Northamptonshire.
Ch. Ch., Middlesex, Parish Register.

POWER, DR. HENRY (d. 1692), York county; son of John Power, Spanish merchant, and his wife ——, daughter of Mr. Jennings, of Kendal, grandson of William Power, and great grandson of Francis Power, of Mossington, Yorkshire.
W. M., I, 210-211; VII, 129.

PRIEST, JOHN (in Virginia 1623), "of Langport in Somersetshire, tayler."
V. M., XIX, 134.

PROCTER, JOHN (in Virginia 1624, &c.); brother of Thomas Procter, citizen of London, who in his will desires to be buried in "great Allhallows," London, and bequeaths lands at Dunmow and Muche Wakeringe, Essex.
V. M., XII, 90-92.

PUREFOY, MRS. LUCY (in Virginia 1629, &c.); wife of Thomas Purefoy, of Elizabeth City county (who named one of his Virginia estates "Drayton"). She was born about 1598, "infra Ranson, Leicestershire."
V. M., I, 417-418.

PUTNAM, THOMAS (d. 1659); son of William Putnam, of Chessam.
V. M., XIV, 305.

RADLEY, THOMAS (d. 1686, Middlesex county); of London.
Ch. Ch., Middlesex, Parish Register.

RAE, ROBERT (1723-1753, Stafford county); son of Robert
Rae, Esq., of Little Govan, near Glasgow, and brother of James
Rae, of Glasgow, merchant.
Essex Records. Va. Hist. Col., XI, 68.

RAMSAY, WILLIAM (1716-1789), Alexandria; a native of
Galloway, Scotland.
Hayden, 88.

RAMSAY, PATRICK (in Virginia 1760, &c.), Blanford; son of
Andrew Ramsay, Provost of Glasgow, Scotland, 1734-5.
Slaughter's Bristol Parish, 210.

RANDOLPH, HENRY (1623-1673), Henrico county and Jamestown; son of William Randolph, of Little Haughton, Northamptonshire, and his wife Dorothy, daughter of Richard Lane,
gent., of Courtenhall, and sister of Sir Richard Lane, Attorney-
General.
V. M., III, 261, &c.

RANDOLPH, WILLIAM (1651-1711), Henrico county; son of
Richard Randolph, of Morton Hall, Warwickshire, and his wife
Elizabeth, daughter of Richard Ryland.
V. M., III, 261, &c.

READE, GEORGE (d. 1671), James City and Gloucester
counties; son of Robert Reade, of Linkenholt, Hampshire (will
dated 1626), and his wife Mildred, daughter of Sir Thomas
Windebank, of Haines' Hall, parish of Hurst, Berkshire.
V. M., IV, 204-205.

REED, ROBERT (d. 1787), Augusta county, 1767, &c.; formerly
of Bellegay, Donegal, Ireland.
Abstracts of Augusta Records, II, 12, 13.

REEVES, GEORGE (d. 1689), Middlesex county; brother of
Charles Reeves, of the parish of Stepney, Middlesex.
V. M., XI, 78.

RENALLS, or REYNOLDS, THOMAS (in Virginia 1658, &c.), Lower Norfolk county; in 1658 his sister, Elizabeth Renalls, was living in Hallyard's Lane, near St. John's Gate, Bristol.
N. E. H. & G. Reg., Vol. 47, p. 354.

RICHARDS, REV. JOHN (1689-1735), Gloucester county; formerly Rector of Nettlestead and Vicar of Teston, Kent.
Meade, I, 354.

ROANE, CHARLES (in Virginia 1664, &c.), Gloucester county; son of Robert Roane, of Chalden, Surrey, gent.
V. M., XVI, 66-70.

ROBERTS, ELIAS (in Virginia 1624, &c.) ; son of Elias Roberts, citizen and merchant-tailor, of London.
W. G., 29.

ROBERTSON, ARCHIBALD (came to Virginia 1746), Prince George county; son of William Robertson, merchant and Baillie of Edinburgh, and brother of Arthur Robertson, chamberlain of Glasgow, 1766, &c.
W. M., V, 185, 186.

ROBINS, JEREMY (in Virginia 1671, &c.) ; son of Jeremy Robins, of St. Martin's in the Fields, London, fringeweaver.
V. M., XV, 63.

ROBINS, OBEDIENCE (1600-1662), Northampton county; born at Brackley, Northamptonshire, April 16, 1600; son of Thomas and Mary (Bulkley) Robins, of Brackley. In 1647 is mention of his brother, Richard Robins, gent., of Longbuckbye, Northamptonshire.
Richmond *Standard,* September 4, 1880, &c.

ROBINS, EDWARD (b. 1602), Northampton county; came to Virginia in 1632; brother of Obedience Robins, preceding.
Richmond *Standard,* September 4, 1880.

ROBINSON, CHRISTOPHER (1645-1692), Middlesex county; son of John and Elizabeth Robinson, of Cleasby, Yorkshire, and brother of John Robinson, Bishop of London.

Roche, James (d. 1652), Isle of Wight county 1649, &c.; died at Queen Camell *alias* East Camell, Somersetshire, England; son of Robert Roche, Vicar of Hilton, Dorset, 1617-1629, and brother of Robert Roche, Vicar of East Camell, 1635-1666.

N. Y. Gen. and Biog. Record, XL, 179, 180.

Rodes, Charles (in Virginia 1695, &c.), New Kent county; son of John Rodes, of Sturton, and grandson of Sir Francis Rodes, Bart. (d. 1645), of Barlborough, Derbyshire.

V. M., VI, 149.

Rodes, Roger (b. about 1604), in Virginia 1623, "of Dowton in Wiltshire," "Mr. Fitzgeffry's servant."

V. M., XIX, 134.

Rogers, Edward (in Virginia 1623), Accomac, "of Porberry in Somersetshire, caryer."

V. M., XIX, 132.

Rolfe, John (1585-1622), son of John and Dorothea (Mason) Rolfe, of Heacham, Norfolk.

V. M., I, 445, &c.

Roper, Thomas (in Virginia 1623), "of Milden in the County of Bedfordshire, gent."

V. M., XIX, 133.

Roscow, William (1661-1700), Warwick county; born at Chorley in the county of Lancaster.

W. M., XIV, 163, 164.

Rose, Rev. Robert (1704-1751), Essex and Albemarle counties; born at Wester Alves, Scotland; son of John Rose (d. 1724) and Margaret Grant (of Whitetree), his wife.

Rose Family Record.

Russell, Thomas (in Virginia 1682, &c.), Lower Norfolk county; formerly of the parish of Kirton, Devon.

Lower Norfolk Records.

Ryding, Thomas (d. shortly before 1693), Accomac county; brother of Hugh Ryding, of Westordby, Lancashire.

Accomac Records.

SANDYS, GEORGE (1577-1643), James City; youngest son of Edwin, Archbishop of York.

V. M., I, 90.

SANFORD, SAMUEL (d. 1710), Accomac county; in will, dated at London, desired to be buried in the parish burying-ground at Avening, Gloucestershire; bequeathed a tenement there, and left £200 for the education of the poor children of Avening.

V. M., April, 1910.

SANFORD, JOHN (d. 1693), Princess Anne county; brother of preceding.

V. M., April, 1910.

SCANDRETT, PUTNAM (in Virginia before 1737); in 1737 of Bristol, merchant.

Essex Records.

SCANDRETT, ISAAC (in Virginia before 1737), Essex county; in 1737 bought lands in Essex county, Va., from Putnam Scandrett, of Bristol, preceding.

Essex Records.

SCARBURGH, EDMUND (d. 1635), Accomac county; son of Henry Scarburgh, gent., of North Walsham, Norfolk.

V. M., IV, 316, 317; XVII, 321, 322. Northampton county (Va.) records cited by the late T. T. Upshur.

SCLATER, JOHN (d. shortly before 1750); "teacher at Col. John Tayloe's in Virginia," Richmond county; son of Robert Sclater, merchant, of Paisley, Scotland, and brother of Jàmes Sclater, "eldest shoemaker" in Paisley.

Essex Records.

SCOTT, REV. ALEXANDER (1686-1738), Stafford county; son of Rev. John Scott, of Dipple parish, Elgin, Morayshire, Scotland.

Hayden, 588, &c.

SCOTT, REV. JAMES (d. 1782), Prince William county; brother of Rev. Alexander Scott, preceding.

Hayden, 593, &c.

SCOVELL, GEORGE, merchant (in another document styled "gentleman"), (in Virginia 1640, &c.); born "infra" the Isle of Purbeck, Dorset; about 39 years old in 1640.
Maryland Archives.

SCRIVENOR, JOSEPH (1722-1772), Williamsburg; born at Oldney, Buckinghamshire.
Va. Hist. Col., VI, 71.

SEDGWICK, WILLIAM (d. 1705, York county); late of "burlen hall in Licking Shire" [Lincolnshire]. (Will.) [The testator did not write the will.]
W. M., VI, 149, 150.

SEDGWICK, ISAAC (in Virginia 1705, &c.); brother of William Sedgwick, preceding.
W. M., VI, 149, 150.

SEMPLE, JAMES (1730-   ), New Kent county; son of Rev. James Semple, minister of Long Dreghorn, Ayshire, Scotland.
Robertson-Taylor Families.

SEMPLE, JOHN (1727-1790), King and Queen county; brother of James Semple, preceding.
W. M., IX, 175.

SEWARD, JOHN (d. 1650), Isle of Wight county; formerly of the parish of St. Leonard, Bistol; bequeathed lands at Bevington and Baddington, Somersetshire.
V. M., X, 406; XIII, 310.

SEXTON, THOMAS (b. about 1605), d. in Virginia 1623, James City; "one of Christ's Hospital."
V. M., XIX, 133, 134.

SHEPHERD, MRS. FRANCES (in Virginia 1693, &c.); wife of Rev. John Shepherd, Middlesex county, and sister of John Robinson, Bishop of London.
Middlesex Records.

SHEPHERD, REV. JOHN (d. 1698), Middlesex county; bequest in his will (1682) to "loving brother living at Parham Hatchetan in the County of Suffolk, England."
Middlesex Records.

SHERWOOD, WILLIAM (d. 1697), Jamestown; "born in the parish of White Chappell near London."
Va. Hist. Col., VI, 95. W. M., XIII, 138, 139.

SIMPSON, JOHN (d. 1688), Middlesex county; of Barking, Essex.
Ch. Ch., Middlesex, Parish Register.

SISSON, THOMAS (in Virginia 1623); "of London, haber-dasher."
V. M., XIX, 132.

SITTERNE, E D W A R D (in Virginia 1688, &c.), Middlesex county; of London.
Ch. Ch., Middlesex, Parish Register.

SKIPWITH, SIR GREY, BART. (d. about 1672), Middlesex county; son of Sir Henry Skipwith, Bart., of Prestwould, Leicestershire.
Middlesex Records. Burke's Peerage and Baronetage.

SKYREN, REV. HENRY (1729-1795), King William and Elizabeth City counties; born at Whitehaven.
Meade, I, 381.

SMITH, AUSTIN (in Virginia 1623), James City; "of London, carpenter."
V. M., XIX, 133, 134.

SMITH, EDWARD (d. 1614); son of Robert Smith. The will of Edward Smith was proved in the diocese of Ely.
V. M., XV, 83, 84.

SMITH, MRS. HANNAH (in Virginia 1680, &c.), Charles City county; wife of Thomas Smith, and daughter of William Daft, wheelwright, of Great Exon, Rutlandshire, and sister, by the

mother's side, of Luke Herbert, of Monk's Kirbie parish, Worcestershire, "who died in Peterborough Minster."
Henrico Records.

SMITH, JOHN (1579-1631); son of George Smith, of Willoughby, Lincolnshire.
Brown's Genesis, II, 1006, &c.

SMITH, JOSEPH (d. 1728), Essex; mentions in his will his deceased brother, John Smith, late of Bidford, merchant, and his brother, James Smith, of Rosse, Ireland.
Essex Records.

SMITH, NICHOLAS (1666-1734), King George county; born in London, son of Nicholas and Efsobah Smith.
W. M., VI, 42.

SMITH, WILLIAM (in Virginia 1666, &c.); brother of Henry Smith, of Watford, Hertfordshire.
V. M., XI, 315.

SOMERVILLE, JAMES (1742-1798), Caroline county; a native of Glasgow.
Hayden, 16.

SOUTHEY, HENRY, ESQ. (came to Virginia after 1622); in 1621 was of Rimpton, Somersetshire.
Proceedings of Virginia Company. Northampton County Records.

SPEKE, THOMAS (1603-1659), Westmoreland county; brother of John Speke, of Bath and Plymouth.
W. M., IV, 41.

SPELMAN, HENRY (in Virginia 1613, &c.); son of Erasmus Spelman, and nephew of Sir Henry Spelman.
V. M., XV, 304-306.

SPELMAN, THOMAS (1601-1627); brother of Francis Spelman, gent., of Truro, Cornwall.
W. G., 72. V. M., I, 195, 196.

SPENCER, MRS. JUDITH (in Virginia 1686, &c.), Middlesex county; of Kent.

Ch. Ch., Middlesex, Parish Register.

SPENCER, NICHOLAS (d. 1689), Westmoreland county; son of Nicholas Spencer, Esq., of Cople, Bedfordshire, and his wife Mary, daughter of Sir Edward Gostwick, Bart., of Willington, Bedfordshire.

V. M., II, 32-34; IV, 451, &c.

SPICER, ARTHUR (d. 1700), Richmond county; brother of John Spicer, and son of Alice Spicer, widow, of Richmond, Surrey.

Richmond County Records.

SPOTSWOOD, ALEXANDER (1676-1740), Spotsylvania county; son of Dr. Robert Spotswood, surgeon in the English army, and grandson of Sir Robert Spotswood, President of the Court of Sessions, Scotland.

Spotswood Letters, I, vii-xv.

SPRING, ROBERT (in Virginia 1680, &c.), York county; in 1679 described as "late of London, merchant."

York County Records.

STEVENS, WILLIAM (in Virginia 1651, &c.), Northampton county; son of John Stevens, of Lebourn, in the parish of Buckingham.

Virginia Carolorum, 207.

STEWART, WILLIAM (d. 1786), Surry county; refers in will (1785) to lands devolving on him in Argyleshire, Scotland, known as Ackinskee.

Surry Records.

STONE, JOHN (in Virginia 1687, &c.), Middlesex county; of Ridgely, Staffordshire.

Ch. Ch., Middlesex, Parish Register.

STONE, MOYSES (b. about 1605, in Virginia 1623), Elizabeth City; "of Longworth in Barkshire."

V. M., XIX, 133, 134.

STONE, WILLIAM (1603-1695), Northampton county 1633, &c.; born in Northamptonshire; nephew of Thomas Stone, haberdasher, of London.

V. M., III, 272, 273.

STORY, THOMAS (in Virginia 1687), &c., Middlesex county; of Colchester, Essex.

Ch. Ch., Middlesex, Parish Register.

STRACHAN, DR. ALEXANDER GLAS (1748-   ), Petersburg; born at Lucar, twelve miles from Edinburgh, July 29, 1748; son of Joseph Strachan, of Edinburgh, and his wife, who was the youngest daughter of Alexander Glas, of Edinburgh, writer to the signet.

Strachan Family Record.

STRACHEY, WILLIAM (d. 1634), Jamestown; son of William Strachey, of Saffron Walden, Essex.

W. M., V, 6; IX, 43.

STRACHEY, WILLIAM (d. 1686), Gloucester county; son of William Strachey, of Saffron Walden, Essex.

W. M., IV, 192-194; V, 6.

STRACHEY, DR. JOHN (1709-1756), King and Queen county; son of John Strachey, of Sutton Court, Chew Magna, Somersetshire.

W. M., IV, 192-194; V, 6.

STRATTON, JOSEPH (d. 1640 or 1641), Nutmeg Quarter and James City county; youngest son of Thomas Stratton, gent, of Shortley, Suffolk, and Dedham, Essex.

Book of Strattons, &c., by Harriet B. Stratton, pp. 42, 75, &c. Putnam's Monthly Historical Magazine, Aug.-Sept., 1896, p. 209.

SUTHERLAND, JOHN (d. 1765), Spotsylvania county; son of John Sutherland, of Winbreck, Orkney Islands, Scotland.

Spotsylvania Records.

SWALE, WILLIAM (d. 1734), formerly of Colchester.

V. M., XI, 145.

SYBERRYE, GEORGE (in Virginia 1623), "of London, Tallow-chandler."
V. M., XIX, 133.

TABERER, JOHN (d. 1654), Isle of Wight county, son of William Taberer, of the county of Derby.
W. M., VII, 221.

TANNER, DANIEL (in Virginia 1640, &c.), Lower Norfolk county. He was married to Charity ——, on November 24, 1614, at St. Paul's Church, Canterbury, and had a son John, baptized October 14, 1627.
N. E. H. & G. Reg., Vol. 47, 354.

TATHAM, WILLIAM (1752-1817, &c.), Richmond, &c.; came to Virginia 1769; son of Rev. Sandford Tatham, and his wife Elizabeth, daughter of Henry Marsden, Esq., of Dennington Hall.
V. M., VIII, 330.

TAYLOE, WILLIAM (d. 1710), Richmond county. There is a letter, dated 1705, from his brother, Joseph Tayloe, to their sister-in-law, "Mrs. Ruth Tayloe, Basinghall Street, London, Under Cover to Mr. Benjamin Tayloe, Bedford Street, Covent Garden, London."
Richmond and Lancaster Records.

TAYLOR, PHILIP (in Virginia 1640, &c.), Accomac county; born in the parish of Marden, Herefordshire; about thirty years old in 1640.
Maryland Archives.

TAYLOR, SAMUEL (in Virginia 1641, &c.); son of John Taylor, of Knightsbridge, Westminster, bricklayer.
V. M., XI, 150.

TAZEWELL, WILLIAM (July 17, 1690-1752), Northampton county; son of James and Anne (Kingswell) Tazewell, of Limington, Somerset.
N. E. H. & G. Reg., Vol. 41, 368.

TEMPLE, JOSEPH (1666-   ), Essex and King and Queen counties; son of William Temple, of Bishopstrow, Wilts, and grandson of John Temple, of Kingston Deverell.

Burke's Landed Gentry (1886). Essex Records.

TEMPLE, REV. PETER, York parish, York county; returned to England, and in 1686 was of "Sible Henigham in the County of Essex, Clerke."

W. M., I, 5.

TERRELL, ROBERT (in Virginia 1647, &c.), York county; citizen and fishmonger, of London; (d. in London 1677). Bequeathed lands in Hampshire. He was son of Robert Terrell, or Tyrrell, of Reading, and great-grandson of George Tyrrell, of Thornton Hall, Bucks.

York Records. V. M., XVI, 190-192. The Tyrrells or Terrells of America (1910).

TERRELL, RICHMOND (in Virginia 1658, &c.), New Kent county; brother of Robert Terrell, preceding.

V. M., XVI, 190-192.

TERRELL, WILLIAM (in Virginia 1670, &c.), New Kent county; brother of Robert Terrell, preceding.

V. M., XVI, 190-192.

THACKER, HENRY (alive 1656-1673, &c.), Lancaster (afterwards Middlesex) county. When on a visit to England in 1656 he stated that "he intended to go to Norwich, and there to remain among his friends."

V. M., XXI, 261. Hayden's Virginia Genealogies, 235-237.

THOMASON, JOHN, "of Virginia," died unmarried, adm. 1677; son of George Thomason, of London, the collector of the "Royal Pamphlets" in the British Museum.

Berry's Sussex Genealogies, 234.

THOMPSON, REV. JOHN (d. 1772), Culpepper county; born at Muckroe Abbey, near Belfast, Ireland.

"Rootes of Rosewall," 33.

THOMPSON, REV. ANDREW (1673-1719), Elizabeth City county; born at Stone Hive, Scotland.

V. M., XI, 145.

THOMPSON, GEORGE (1603-1694), in Virginia 1624, &c.; son of Ralph Thompson, gent., of Walton, Hertfordshire.

W. G., 1023. V. M., I, 189-190.

THOMPSON, MAURICE (d. 1676), in Virginia 1620, &c.; brother of George Thompson, preceding.

W. G., 1023. V. M., I, 188-189.

THOMPSON, PAUL (1611-   ), in Virginia 1624, &c.; brother of George Thompson, preceding.

V. M., I, 190.

THOMPSON, WILLIAM (1614-   ), in Virginia 1624, &c.; brother of George Thompson, preceding.

THOMPSON, RICHARD (1613-1657), Northumberland County; born in the city of Norwich.

W. M., XVII, 58.

THOMPSON, STEVENS (d. 1714), Williamsburg; son of Sir William Thompson, of London, Sergeant-at-Law (who was knighted October 31, 1689).

W. M., III, 154-155.

THORPE, MRS. CATHERINE (d. 1714), wife of Thomas Thorpe, of James City county, and daughter of Francis Seaton, of Pole-brook, Northamptonshire.

V. M., IV, 135.

THORPE, GEORGE (d. 1622), son of Nicholas Thorpe, of Wans-well Court, Gloucestershire.

W. M., IX, 209, 210.

THORNBOROUGH, THORNBURY, ROWLAND (in Virginia before 1696, d. in Maryland 1696), Rappahannock county; in will leaves estate, in case of death of sons s. p., to his next of kin, the

Thornboroughs at Hampsfield, Lancashire. Lived first in Virginia, and removed to Maryland, where he died.

Maryland Calendar of Wills, II, 111. W. M., III, 71.

THOROUGHGOOD, ADAM (1602-1641), Lower Norfolk county; brother of Sir John Thoroughgood, and son of William Thoroughgood, of Grimston, Commissary of the Bishop of Norwich.

V. M., II, 414-416.

THOROUGHGOOD, MRS. SARAH (d. 1657), wife of Adam Thoroughgood of Lower Norfolk county, and daughter of Robert Offley of London, and his wife Anne, daughter of Sir Edward Osborne, Lord Mayor of London.

V. M., V, 435; XII, 201, 202.

THROCKMORTON, ALBION (1674-   ), Gloucester county; son of John Throckmorton, of Ellington, Huntingdonshire.

W. M., III, 46-49; V, 54, 55. V. M., VIII, 84, &c.

THROCKMORTON, JOHN (1633-1678), Gloucester county; son of Robert Throckmorton, of Ellington, Huntingdonshire.

W. M., III, 46-49; V, 54, 55. W. M., VIII, 84, &c.

THROCKMORTON, GABRIEL (1665-1737), Gloucester county son of John Throckmorton, of Ellington, Huntingdonshire.

W. M., V, 54, 55; III, 46-49. W. M., VIII, 84, &c.

THRUSTON, EDWARD (1638-   ), Warwick county; son of John Thruston, Chamberlain of Bristol.

W. M., IV, 25, 116, &c.

THRUSTON, MALACHY (1637-1699), Princess Anne county; son of John Thruston, Chamberlain of Bristol.

W. M., IV, 25-27.

THRUSTON, ROBERT (d. 1678), "late resident at St. Pulchers [St. Sepulcher's] parish, London, armourer."

V. M., XVII, 69.

TIRREY, JOHN, gent. (1649-1700), Surry county; born in London.

V. M., VII, 211.

TOOKER, HENRY (1673-1737), Surry county; son of Henry Tooker, Esq., of Winton [Winchester] in the county of Southampton.
V. M., VII, 211.

TORKINGTON, JOSEPH (in Virginia 1652, &c., d. 1652); brother of Samuel Torkington, citizen and grocer of London.
Will of Joseph Torkington, P. C. C. Brent, 320.

TOWLSON, JOHN (d. shortly before 1661), Northampton county; uncle of William Towlson, husbandman, of the parish of Hearne, Kent.
Northampton Records.

TOWNSHEND, MRS. FRANCES (in Virginia 1640, &c.); wife of Richard Townshend, of York county, and sister of Robert Baldwin, gent., of London, and William Baldwin, of Glassthorn, Northamptonshire.
W. M., XII, 249.

TOWNSHEND, MRS. MARY, wife of Robert Townshend (d. 1675) of Stafford county, and daughter of Needham Langhorne, of Newton Brownshall, Northamptonshire.
W. M., XII, 245, 299. V. M., XI, 146.

TRAHERNE, RICHARD (in Virginia 1658, &c.); brother of William Traherne, of St. Clements Danes, Middlesex, chandler.

TREVETHAN, SAMPSON (in Virginia 1699, &c.), Lower Norfolk county; in 1715 returned to England, and was of Laragon, Penzance, Cornwall.
Lower Norfolk Records.

TUCKER, DANIEL (in Virginia 1608, &c.); son of George Tucker, Esq., of Milton, Kent. At a much later date St. George Tucker and other descendants of George Tucker, of Milton, emigrated to Virginia from Bermuda and Barbadoes.
Brown's Genesis, II, 1033. V. M., XVII, 394.

TUCKER, WILLIAM (1589-1644), Elizabeth City county, in Virginia 1610-32. In will styled of—"St. Dunstans in the East, City of London, Esquire," and names "Brothers" Edmund

Smyth, Esq., Maurice Thomson, merchant, and Elias Roberts, merchant, and Cousin Thos. Downey, citizen and merchant of London.

V. M., XXII, 267.

TYLER, THOMAS, founder (in Virginia 1722, &c.), Hanover county; in 1727, by deed conveyed his plantation, &c., in Spotsylvania county, to his son, Charles Tyler, residing in Hopton-Wafer parish, Shropshire.

Spotsylvania County Records.

TYRE, MRS. REBECCA (in Virginia 1708, &c.); wife of James Tyre, of New Kent county, and daughter of John Sergeant, of Bermondsey, Surrey, weaver.

UNDERHILL, JOHN (d. 1673), York county; born in the city of Worcester.

W. M., II, 85. V. M., XVI, 94.

UNETT, JOHN (in Virginia 1622, &c.); son of John Unett, of St. Ann's, Blackfriars, London, whose nearest kindred lived at Ashellworth, Gloucestershire.

V. M., XI, 316.

UPSHUR, ARTHUR (1623-1709), Northampton county; "born in ye County of Essex in ye Kingdom of England."

W. M., III, 256.

VANSOLDT, ABRAHAM (in Virginia 1665); son of Elizabeth Vansoldt, widow, of Whitegate Alley in the parish of Buttolphs, Bishopsgate, London.

V. M., XVI, 198.

VAUGHAN, HOWELL (d. in Virginia before 1686); formerly of Lloydarth, County Montgomery.

N. E. H. & G. Reg., Vol. 59, 109.

VAULX, JAMES (d. 1682), York county; formerly merchant of London.

W. M., III, 153.

VAULX, ROBERT (1651-1685), Westmoreland county; son of Robert and Elizabeth Vaulx, of London.

W. M., IV, 42.

VIZER, HENRY (in Virginia 1667, &c.) ; son of Robert Vizer, of Bristol, formerly of Dublin.

V. M., XI, 367.

VYNN, JEREMY (d. 1687), Middlesex county; of Norwich.

Ch. Ch., Middlesex, Parish Register.

WAGENER, PETER (in Virginia 1739, &c.), Fairfax county; born at Sisted, Essex, August 5, 1717; son of Rev. Peter Wagener, Rector of Sisted.

V. M., VIII, 60; XVI, 217.

WAGGAMAN, MRS. MARGARET, wife of Jonathan Waggaman (who d. in Virginia about 1725), and daughter of William Elliott, Esq., of Wells, and of York Buildings, St. Martin's in the Fields, London.

V. M., XIII, 95, 99. W. M., XVII, 300, 301.

WALKER, JOHN (d. 1745), Middlesex county; son of John Walker, of Ashborne-in-the-Peak, Derbyshire.

V. M., I, 470, 471. Robinson Pedigree.

WALKER, RICHARD (d. 1726), Middlesex county; brother of John Walker, of Ashborne-in-the-Peak, Derbyshire.

V. M., I, 470.

WALLACE, DAVID (d. before March 14, 1750), "planter in James River." Had a sister Patience Wallace, apparently dead in 1750, who married John Morrison, merchant, in Stonehaven, Scotland.

Spotsylvania Records, 186.

WALLACE, REV. JAMES (1677-1712), Elizabeth City county; native of Erroll, Perthshire, Scotland.

W. M., III, 168.

WALLACE, DR. MICHAEL (1719-1767), King George county; son of William Wallace, of Galrigs, merchant, and nephew of John Wallace, of Elderslee (or Ellerslie), Renfrewshire, Scotland.

Hayden, 687-701.

WADLEY, THOMAS (b. 1633, in Virginia 1661, &c.), York county; son and heir of Thomas Wadley, deceased, late citizen and merchant tailor of London, whose will was dated Sept. 26, 1659. Thos. Wadley the younger sold in 1661 a tenement "called the Rowbuck" in the parish of St. Matthew, Friday Street, which had been left him by his father.
York County Records.

WALTON, THOMAS (d. 1670), Isle of Wight county; his next of kin, after his children, lived at Castor near Peterborough, Northamptonshire.
W. M., VII, 237.

WARDEN, THOMAS (in Virginia 1623), Accomac county; "of Ely in Hampshire, husbandman."
V. M., XIX, 132.

WARKMAN, MARK (in Virginia 1684, &c.), New Kent county; son of Mark Gloucester *als*. Warkman, citizen and grocer, of London.
V. M., XI, 308.

WARKMAN, ROBERT (in Virginia 1670, &c.); brother of Mark Gloucester *als*. Warkman, citizen and grocer, of London.
V. M., XI, 308.

WARNETT, THOMAS (in Virginia 1629, &c.), James City county; son of John Warnett, of Southwark, Surrey.
W. G., 40, 41.

WASHINGTON, JOHN (1631-1677), Westmoreland county; son of Rev. Lawrence Washington, Rector of Purleigh, Essex.
W. G., 352-404.

WASHINGTON, LAWRENCE (1635-1677), Rappahannock county; brother of John Washington, preceding.
W. G., 352-404. W. M., I, 184-188.

WATERS, EDWARD, gent. (1584-1630), Elizabeth City county; will dated at Great Hornmead, Hertfordshire; names in it his brother, John Waters, of Middleham, Yorkshire.
V. M., I, 92; II, 179.

WATERS, JOHN (d. 1694), Rappahannock county; son of Mrs. Ann Waters, widow, of St. Sepulchre's, London (in 1697).
V. M., XI, 305.

WATKIN, GEORGE (d. 1673), Surry county. In his will (1673) he desires "to be buried in a decent manner in the Chancell of ye Church of Lawnes Creek [Va.] as my predecessors have been in ye p'rsh Churches where they dwelt"; gives legacies to his uncle, Charles Barham [in Virginia], and to his cousin, Christopher Watkin, of "White Hart Court, in Long Lane, London."
Surry Records.

WATTS, WILLIAM (in Virginia 1641, &c.); son of Cornelius Watts, of St. Cuthberts, in the city of Wells, vintner.
V. M., XIII, 307.

WATTS, WILLIAM (in Virginia 1641, &c.); formerly fishmonger, of London.
N. E. H. & G. Reg., Vol. 61, 199.

WEAVER, SAMUEL (b. 1605, in Virginia 1623), Martin's Hundred, "of London."
V. M., XIX, 133, 134.

WEBB, GEORGE (in Virginia 1728, &c.), New Kent county; son of Conrad Webb, of London, merchant.
Webb Family Bible.

WEBB, GILES (d. 1713), Henrico county; brother of Thomas Webb, of the city of Gloucester, gent. (who was alive 1716).
Henrico County Records.

WEBB, STEPHEN (in Virginia 1642, &c.), James City and Surry counties; born at Breshley, Worcestershire, and baptized there September 1, 1598; son of Stephen and Ann Webb.
V. M., III, 57.

WEDDERBURN, DAVID (1682-   ), lived on York River; son of Peter Wedderburn, of Donside (b. 1652), and grandson of Sir Alexander Wedderburn, of Blackness, Forfarshire, Scotland (1610-1676).
Burke's Peerage and Bartonetage; Wedderburn of Balinden.

WELCH, REUBEN (d. in or before 1729), lived on Rappahannock River in Virginia; brother of Thomas Welch, of Tottenham High Cross, Middlesex, England (alive 1729), and had another brother living at Walthamstow.

York County Records.

WEST, FRANCIS (1586-1634); son of Thomas, 2nd Lord Delaware.

V. M., II, 308; XI, 359.

WEST, JOHN (1590-1659), York county; brother of Francis West, preceding.

V. M., I, 423. Foster's Oxford Matriculations. W. M., II, 152.

WEST, JOHN (in Virginia 1623), James City; "of Witley in Surrey, husbandman."

V. M., XIX, 133, 134.

WEST, NATHANIEL (1592-   ), in Virginia 1617-1625, &c.; brother of Francis West, preceding.

Brown's Genesis and First Republic.

WEST, THOMAS (d. in Virginia 1724), "of London, cooper."
V. M., XIX, 133, 134.

WEST, WILLIAM (d. before 1686); son of William West, yeoman, of Eaton, Berkshire (will 1686).

W. G., 626.

WESTCOATE, MRS. ELIZABETH (in Virginia 1659, &c.); daughter of George Bartlett, citizen and pavior, of London.

V. M., XI, 149.

WETHERS, ERASMUS (in Virginia 1677, &c., died in or before 1697), Middlesex county. There is mention that the will of Erasmus Snelling, citizen and ironmonger, of London, dated January 18, 1671, and proved P. C. C., gave legacies to said Erasmus Wethers, of Virginia, Erasmus Maddocks, of East Greenwich in the county of Kent, woodmonger, and Margaret, wife of Richard Thomas, of Deptford.

Middlesex Records.

WHARTON, RICHARD (d. 1713), Williamsburg; son of William Wharton, gent., of Wasteby near Wharton, Westmoreland.
W. G., 1094.

WHARTON, DR. THOMAS, apothecary (d. 1745), Williamsburg; son of Robert Wharton, Alderman, of Durham.
York County Records.

WHITAKER, REV. ALEXANDER (1585-1617), Henrico county; son of William Whitaker, D. D., Master of Emanuel College, Cambridge.
V. M., XI, 147, 148.

WHITAKER, MRS. MARY, wife of Captain Jabez Whitaker (in Virginia 1622, &c.), and daughter of Sir John Bourchier, of Lambeth, Surrey (d. 1626), uncle of the Regicide.
V. M., I, 295. P. C. C. Act Book.

WHITE, AGNES (d. 1757), wife of Robert White, of Spotsylvania county; had two sisters in Scotland, Margaret Ray and Jean Macklenahan, whose maiden name was Johnson, and an uncle, William Maxwell, living in Rutherglen near Glasgow.
Spotsylvania Records, p. 15.

WHITE, JOHN (in Virginia 1670, &c.); nephew of John White, Vicar of Cherton *als*. Cheirton (Cherrington), Wiltshire.
V. M., XI, 367-368.

WHITE, JOHN (in Virginia 1676, &c.); brother of William White, citizen and haberdasher, of London.
V. M., XV, 64.

WHITE, REV. WILLIAM (d. 1678), York and Lancaster counties; brother of Rev. Jeremiah White, of England.
Lancaster Records.

WHITEHEAD, JOHN (in Virginia 1701), indentured servant; of Wixon, Lancashire.
Essex Records.

WHITEHEAD, JONATHAN (d. 1686), Middlesex county; of Southwark, London.
Ch. Ch., Middlesex, Parish Register.

WHITLOCK, MRS. —— (in Virginia 1677, &c.); daughter of John Hearne (dead in 1677) and niece of Sir Nathaniel Hearne, Knt., and Alderman, of London.
V. M., XV, 184, 185.

WILCOCKS or WILCOX, JOHN (d. 1622), "late of Plymouth."
V. M., II, 77, 78. W. G., 3.

WILLIAMS, DANIEL (d. 1721), formerly of Stepney, Middlesex.
Will, Consistory Court of London.

WILLIAMS, GEORGE (d. 1686), Middlesex county; of Kent.
Ch. Ch., Middlesex, Parish Register.

WILLIAMS, JOHN (in Virginia 1686, &c.), Middlesex county; of Oxfordshire.
Ch. Ch., Middlesex, Parish Register.

WILLIAMS, MRS. RACHEL (1718-1746), wife of Thomas Williams of Petersburg, and daughter of "Mr. John Freeman and Mary his wife of Wilsey in Gloster."
W. M., V, 239.

WILLIAMS, THOMAS (d. 1686), Middlesex county; of Herefordshire.
Ch. Ch., Middlesex, Parish Register.

WILLIAMS, THOMAS (1702-1763), Petersburg; born in St. James' parish, London.
W. M., V, 239.

WILLIAMS, REV. WILLIAM (in Virginia about 1690), James City county; son of Walter Williams, and grandson of Roger Williams, of the Gore near Brecknock.
V. M., X, 107.

WILLIAMSON, ROGER (in Virginia 1646, &c.); brother of Richard Williamson, citizen and merchant tailor, of London.
V. M., XV, 181.

WILLIS, MRS. ANNE (1695-1727), Gloucester county; wife of Francis Willis, daughter of Edward Rich and niece of Elias Rich, Esq., of St. Paul's, Covent Garden, London.

W. G., 1086. W. M., III, 182, 188.

WILLIS, FRANCIS (d. 1691), Gloucester county; a native of the parish of St. Algate, City of Oxford.

W. G., 239. W. M., V, 24-27.

WILLISON, JAMES (1751-1787), Surry county; born at Port Glasgow, Scotland; son of John Willison and Margaret Dunbar his wife.

Willison Bible Record.

WILSON, RICHARD (in Virginia 1639, &c.); son of Richard Wilson, citizen and draper, of London.

W. G., 830.

WILLOUGHBY, HENRY (1626-1685), Rappahannock county; born at Stewkley, England; son of George Willoughby, Esq., and grandson of Sir Ambrose Willoughby, Knt., of Malton, Gloucestershire, who was 2nd son of Charles, 2nd Lord Willoughby of Parham.

Collins' Peerage. Rappahannock County Records.

WINGATE, ROGER, ESQ. (d. about 1641); of Bedfordshire.

W. M., I, 84. Keith's Ancestry of Benjamin Harrison. Visitation of Bedfordshire (Harlean Society).

WINGATE, MRS. DOROTHY (in Virginia 1640, &c.); wife of Roger Wingate, and before of Lewis Burwell, and daughter of William Bedell, of Catworth, Huntingdonshire.

Keith's Ancestry of Benjamin Harrison, 34, 35.

WITHAM, CUTHBERT (in Virginia 1665, &c.); son of William Witham, of Yorkshire.

W. M., II, 27.

WITHE, SIMON (in Virginia 1623), Elizabeth City; "of London, bricklayer."

V. M., XIX, 132.

WITTON, RICHARD (d. 1728), Chesterfield county 1752, &c., afterwards in Mecklenburg; had (in 1771) a sister, Lydia Deykin, living at Walsale, Staffordshire.
Mecklenburg Records.

WOODHOUSE, HENRY (1607-1655), Lower Norfolk county; son of Henry Woodhouse, and grandson of Sir Henry Woodhouse, of Waxham, Norfolk, and his wife Ann, daughter of Sir Nicholas Bacon.
W. M., I, 227-232; II, 262-264; V, 41-44. V. M., XIII, 203; XV, 363.

WOOLARD, WILLIAM (in Virginia 1671, &c.), Isle of Wight county; formerly of Harwich, Essex.
W. M., VII, 228.

WOORY, JOSEPH (in Virginia 1669, &c.), Isle of Wight county; nephew of Sir John Yeamans, Bart., of Barbadoes (formerly of Bristol).
W. M., VII, 237.

WORMELEY, CHRISTOPHER (in Virginia 1637, &c., d. before October, 1649), York county; son of Christopher Wormeley, of Adwick le Street, Yorkshire.
Miss Wormeley's Memoir of Admiral Wormeley. Hayden's Virginia Genealogies, 230, 231.

WORMELEY, RALPH (d. 1651), York and Lancaster counties; brother of Christopher Wormeley, preceding.
Miss Wormeley's Memoir of Admiral Wormeley. Hayden's Virginia Genealogies, 230, 231.

WYATT, SIR DUDLEY (d. 1651), York county; living there March 29, 1650; will dated Sept. 25, 1651, pro. in Secretary's office at Jamestown. He was in England and France in the service of Charles I in 1646.
York County Records. Clarendon (ed. Oxford 1839) V, 339, 349.

WYATT, REV. HAWTE (1594-1638), James City; in Virginia 1621-25; son of Sir George Wyatt, of Boxley, Kent, and his

wife Jane, daughter of Sir Thomas Finch, of Eastwell, Kent.
V. M., II, 177-180; XVI, 204, 205. W. M., X, 59-60; XII, 35-45, 111-116.

WYATT, EDWARD (in Virginia 1662, &c.), Middle Plantation and Gloucester county; son of Rev. Hawte Wyatt, of Boxley, Kent.
V. M., II, 179-180; XVI, 204, 205. W. M., X, 59-61; XII, 35-45, 111-116.

WYATT, GEORGE (in Virginia 1662 &c.), Middle Plantation; brother of Edward Wyatt, preceding.
Same references.

WYNNE, ROBERT (d. 1670), Charles City county; bequeathed farm in "Whitestaple" parish, Kent, called Linbet Banckes; two houses in Canterbury in St. Mildred's parish; three houses and one oatmeal mill in Dover Lane, without St. Georges, Canterbury.
V. M., XIV, 173, 174.

YALDEN, EDWARD, in Isle of Wight county, 1669, &c.; son of Anthony Yalden, of Winchester.
Isle of Wight Records.

YATES, CHARLES (1728-1807), Fredericksburg; son of Rev. Francis Yates, Rector of Grangrave, Yorkshire (d. 1798), and Ann Orfear his wife.
W. Va. Hist. Mag., July, 1892, 44-47.

YEARDLEY, SIR GEORGE (d. 1627), James City; son of Ralph Yeardley, citizen and merchant tailor, of London.
W. G., 189. V. M., I, 85, 86.

YEO, GEORGE (d. 1743), Elizabeth City county; bequeathed certain tenements in the Borough of Hatherley, Devon, called Wadlands and Finch Park.
W. M., IV, 61.

YEO, HUGH (d. about 1680), Northampton county; brother of Justinian Yeo, of Harton, in the parish of Hartland, Devon.
W. M., IX, 125.

YEO, JUSTINIAN (in Virginia 1693, &c.), Accomac county; formerly of Harton, in the parish of Hartlands, Devon; brother of Hugh Yeo, preceding.

Accomac Records.

YOUELL, THOMAS (d. in or before 1657), Northumberland and Lancaster counties; lived before in Maryland; born in the parish of Wilbarsonne, Northamptonshire; in 1640 was 22 years old.

Maryland Archives. Hayden's Virginia Genealogies, 332-334.

YUILLE, JOHN (1719-1746), Williamsburg; son of John Yuille, of Darleith, Scotland.

Va. Hist. Col., XI, 67.

ZOUCH, SIR JOHN (d. 1639), formerly of Codnor, Derbyshire.

V. M., XII, 87-88, 429, &c.

ZOUCH, JOHN (in Virginia 1639, &c.); son of Sir John Zouch, of Codnor, Derbyshire, and of Virginia.

V. M., XII, 87-88, 429, &c.